HOW TO BLOW UP A PIPELINE

HOW TO BLOW
UP A PIPELINE

Learning to Fight in a World on Fire

Andreas Malm

VERSO

London • New York

First published by Verso 2021
© Andreas Malm 2021

7 9 10 8

Verso
UK: 6 Meard Street, London W1F 0EG
US: 20 Jay Street, Suite 1010, Brooklyn, NY 11201
versobooks.com

Verso is the imprint of New Left Books

ISBN-13: 978-1-83976-025-9
ISBN-13: 978-1-83976-027-3 (UK EBK)
ISBN-13: 978-1-83976-026-6 (US EBK)

British Library Cataloguing in Publication Data
A catalogue record for this book is available from the British Library

Library of Congress Cataloging-in-Publication Data
A catalog record for this book is available from the Library of Congress
Library of Congress Control Number: 2020936555

Typeset in Adobe Garamond by Hewer Text UK Ltd, Edinburgh
Printed and bound by CPI Group (UK) Ltd, Croydon CR0 4YY

Contents

PREFACE

No More Excuses for Passivity

The manuscript for this book was completed before the coronavirus known as COVID-19 struck. As I write these words, the pandemic is killing some 2,000 individuals worldwide per day. It also has political victims, one of the first being the climate movement, whose high-flying popular mobilisations were punctured in an instant by the outbreak. The climate strikes that swept the globe in 2019 have been put on hold. Just before most of Europe went into complete lockdown, I met comrades in Amsterdam who had spent the past year preparing for one of the most exciting mass actions yet, called Shell Must Fall: a militant disruption of the annual shareholders' meeting of Shell, advertised by the activists as the last meeting of the kind. Despondently, they realised that the action would not go ahead. In Berlin, where I write these words, the coalition at the centre of the movement, Ende Gelände, which had similarly grand plans for 2020, has had to call off its assemblies; the two-week-long camp in the centre of the city planned by Extinction Rebellion has been cancelled. Before COVID-19, the climate movement was soaring to ever-greater heights of mass participation, but the fuel of every social movement has suddenly become so insalubrious as to be outlawed: crowds. One could be forgiven for feeling that the fate of the planet is in the hands of some malevolent celestial force.

But world capitalism has also had to close its shops like never before. Therein lies an opportunity. Emissions will plunge – again, just like after the financial crisis of 2008, for reasons entirely unrelated to climate policy – which in itself is a good thing. Taboos against interfering with private property have been broken. If a pandemic can induce governments to take emergency actions, why can't a climate breakdown that threatens to kill off the very life-support systems of the planet do the same? After this, there can be no more excuses for passivity.

This is not to say that aggressive climate measures will happen automatically, that the curfews and closed industries and paused airports will necessarily extend into a transition away from fossil fuels. We should rather expect the opposite: business-as-usual bouncing back as soon as the pandemic dies down. The car companies will itch to restart production, the airlines to fly again, the oil and gas companies to profit from prices rising anew. If the corona crisis constitutes an opportunity for climate mitigation, it can be realised *only if acted upon*.

And so the climate movement might be hibernating in quarantine for the moment, just like everybody else, but as soon as this particular emergency regime is relaxed, it must spring forth with all the vigour it can muster. Whether time has been lost or gained on balance, the struggle against climate catastrophe will be as urgent as ever. A pandemic may course through the world for a couple of years. It could peter out. It might be combatted with a vaccine. But global heating will *only become progressively worse until the moment greenhouse gas emissions cease* and drawdown of CO_2 from the atmosphere commences. Nothing indicates that this will happen by itself – that fossil capital will die a natural death – which means that the climate movement will be in even greater historical demand one or two or five years from now. The tactical choices this book ponders will then reappear.

I should like to believe that the arguments put forth here have a decent chance of surviving this pandemic, insofar as the movement rebounds. The need for militancy is unlikely to be diminished. It is thus my hope that the discussion in the following pages will be of some value for the movement in its post-corona phase – or even in a phase contemporaneous with COVID-19 or some other future pandemic. Sabotage, after all, is not incompatible with social distancing.

Berlin, late March 2020

I

Learning from Past Struggles

On the last day of the negotiations, we geared up for our most daring action yet. We had been camping out in a shabby gymnasium in the eastern part of the city for a week. My friends and I had arrived there on a decrepit bus – on the road, in the middle of the night, the exhaust pipe fell off – but when we spread out on the yard of the sports centre we felt the rush of entering an alternative world: a place where business-as-usual had been suspended. A communal kitchen served vegan food. Assemblies were open to anyone with something to say. During one work-shop, a man from Bangladesh outlined the devastating consequences of rising sea levels for his country; at another, delegates from small island states came to voice their distress as well as their support. My friends and I secured an audience with our environmental minister and urged her to ratchet up ambitions. The science, after all, had been clear for a long time by now.

One day we poured out of subway stations and onto a busy junction in the middle of the city and blocked the traffic with banners calling for emissions to be slashed. Activists played guitars and violins while others danced; some juggled; some handed out sunflower seeds to irate motorists. We had no intention of confronting the police or anyone else; we'd rather get arrested than throw a bottle or stone. The next day, we flooded a thoroughfare with an elaborate street theatre. Dressed up as trees, flowers and animals, we laid down on the tarmac to be run over by a vehicle built of cardboard and wood to symbolise business-as-usual. Striding through the flattened crowd, protesters in UN delegate costumes carried signs saying 'Blah-Blah-Blah' and did nothing.

And now it was the final day of the negotiations. Hired buses drove all 500 of us close to the venue. On signal, we marched to the building and tried to prevent the delegates from leaving by locking ourselves to the gates with chains and lying down on the ground, all the while chanting: 'No more blah-blah-blah . . . Action now! No more blah-blah-blah . . . Action now!'

This happened in 1995. The scene was COP1, the very first in the annual series of UN climate summits, in Berlin. The delegates snuck out through a backdoor. Since then, total annual CO_2 emissions in the world have grown by some 60 per cent. In the year of that summit, the combustion of fossil fuels pumped more than six gigatons of carbon into the atmosphere; in 2018, the figure passed ten. In the twenty-five years after the delegates left, more carbon was released from underground stocks than in the seventy-five years before they met.

Since COP1, the US has set off a boom in fossil fuel extraction, once again becoming the world's top producer of oil and gas; home to the largest network of pipelines, it has added upwards of 800,000 miles, multiplying and elongating the high-pressure hoses for dousing fuel on the fire. Germany has continued to dig up nearly 200 million tons of brown coal – the dirtiest of all fossil fuels – every year. The open pit mines expand relentlessly, forests and villages being torn down so the sooty bowls can stretch beyond the horizon and the excavators can shovel up more soft rock to be set on fire. Since COP1, my home country, Sweden, has initiated one of the largest infrastructure projects in its history: a massive 'ring road' highway. Nothing extraordinary, just another highway. Coiling around Stockholm, it is meant to carry more cars spewing out ever more millions of tons of the noxious element. In April 1995, the month COP1 came to an end, the atmospheric concentration of CO_2 stood at 363 parts per million. In April 2018, it was higher than 410 ppm.

A cloud of smoke billows across Siberia as I write these words. It originates from wildfires of unprecedented extent and ferocity within the Arctic Circle; for weeks, the flames have been sweeping through what should be the coldest forests on Earth and sending up plumes into one giant formation of soot. The cloud is now larger than the territory of the European Union. Before it dissipates, swathes of the Amazon catch fire and turn to ash at a pace never registered before.

To say that the signals have fallen on the deaf ears of the ruling classes of this world would be an understatement. If these classes ever had any senses, they have lost them all. They are not perturbed by the smell from the blazing trees. They do not worry at the sight of islands sinking; they do not run from the roar of the approaching hurricanes; their fingers never need to touch the stalks from withered harvests; their mouths do not become sticky and dry after a day with nothing to drink. To appeal to their reason and common sense would evidently be futile. The commitment to the endless accumulation of capital wins out every time. After the past three decades, there can be no doubt that the ruling classes are constitutionally incapable of responding to the catastrophe in any other way than by expediting it; of their own accord, under their inner compulsion, they can do nothing but burn their way to the end.

And so we are still here. We erect our camps of sustainable solutions. We cook our vegan food and hold our assemblies. We march, we block, we stage theatres, we hand over lists of demands to ministers, we chain ourselves, we march the next day too. We are still perfectly, immaculately peaceful. There are more of us now, by orders of magnitude. There is another pitch of desperation in our voices; we talk of extinction and no future. And still business continues very much as usual.

At what point do we escalate? When do we conclude that the time has come to also try something different?

graves today in Dominica!' he exclaimed. 'We buried loved ones yesterday and I am sure that as I return home tomorrow, we shall discover additional fatalities. Our homes are flattened! Our buildings are roofless! Our crops are uprooted! Where there was green there is now only dust and dirt.' Aptly summing up the science, Skerrit explained to the world's congregated leaders that the heat in the ocean functions as a fuel load for storms, supercharging them and turning them into weapons of mass destruction. The heat was not generated by Caribbean peoples. An island almost exclusively inhabited by the descendants of slaves and a sliver of an indigenous population, Dominica remains impoverished, a world away from New York City or London, responsible for a level of fossil fuel combustion so miniscule that it alone would have left no trace on the planet. 'The war has come to us!' Skerrit cried out, struggling to contain the pain. 'We are shouldering the consequences of the actions of others. Actions that endanger our very existence . . . and all for the enrichment of a few elsewhere.' He made a desperate plea to his audience. 'We need action' – action, that is, to cut emissions – 'and we need it NOW!!' He probably knew on what kind of ears his words would fall. His war imagery was apt; like a precision-guided missile, Hurricane Maria departed Dominica and continued towards Puerto Rico, where the scenes were repeated, flooding and mudslides shattering villages and killing people in droves. The government put the death toll at sixty-four, but several independent research teams demonstrated that the real

figure was somewhere between 3,000 and 6,000. No similar assessments were conducted for Dominica.

Two weeks before Maria, as a comment on the ongoing hyperactive hurricane season, one publication that
had long taken an interest in climate change, the *London
Review of Books*, pulled out essays on the topic from its
archives and sent them to subscribers. The first was written by the British novelist and essayist John Lanchester. It
begins:

> It is strange and striking that climate change activists
> have not committed any acts of terrorism. After all,
> terrorism is for the individual by far the modern
> world's most effective form of political action, and
> climate change is an issue about which people feel
> just as strongly as about, say, animal rights. This is
> especially noticeable when you bear in mind the ease
> of things like blowing up petrol stations, or vandalis-
> ing SUVs. In cities, SUVs are loathed by everyone
> except the people who drive them; and in a city the
> size of London, a few dozen people could in a short
> space of time make the ownership of these cars effec-
> tively impossible, just by running keys down the side
> of them, at a cost to the owner of several thousand
> pounds a time. Say fifty people vandalising four cars
> each every night for a month: six thousand trashed
> SUVs in a month and the Chelsea tractors would
> soon be disappearing from our streets. So why don't
> these things happen? Is it because the people who

feel strongly about climate change are simply too nice, too educated, to do anything of the sort? (But terrorists are often highly educated.) Or is it that even the people who feel most strongly about climate change on some level can't quite bring themselves to believe in it?

These words were penned ten years before the hurricane season of 2017. They were written before floods inundated a fifth of Pakistan and ruined the lives of some 20 million people, before Cyclone Nargis killed a couple of hundred thousand in Myanmar, before Typhoon Haiyan killed more than six thousand in the Philippines, before Cyclone Idai devastated central Mozambique, before Matthew, Isaac, Irma, Dorian, before the droughts settled on Central America and took hold of Iran and Afghanistan, before mudslides killed more than a thousand in the capital of Sierra Leone and monsoon-like rains washed away hundreds of villages in Peru and the thermometer regularly reached levels barely endurable by the human body in the Persian Gulf, before uncountable other disasters – some reaching deep into the global North: heatwaves roasting Europe for two consecutive summers, the worst wildfires in the history of California – all formed in the cauldron of an overheated world. And still the same conditions prevail. They are puzzling. At least five factors make them so.

First, the magnitude of what is at stake: close to all living beings in heaven and on earth. Second, the ubiquity of potential targets in advanced capitalist countries. A petrol station or an SUV is rarely more than a stone's throw away – a factor absent, crucially, in countries like Dominica, where emissions sources can be few and far between. Third, the facility with which such things could be taken out of service; no very complicated instruments would have to be employed. Fourth, the awareness of the structure and dimensions of the crisis (considerably more widespread now than when Lanchester's essay was published), weighing rather heavier on people's minds than an issue like animal rights. To these easily ascertainable factors, Lanchester added a fifth of a speculative nature: the efficacy of a campaign to take out the most emissions-intensive devices. We do not know if the results are guaranteed, because no such campaigns have yet, as of this writing, been undertaken. On the other hand, one could adduce a sixth factor that is always fully evident: the enormity of the injustice being perpetrated.

All in all, this makes it strange and striking indeed that the kind of actions described by Lanchester have not been taken. It is a paradox: call it simply 'Lanchester's paradox'. It registers part of the general deficit of action in response to climate breakdown. It captures a form of inaction within the world of activism itself. There is a relation between it and the blah-blah-blah of politicians.

The climate movement in the global North has undergone several cycles of intense activity, each on a larger scale than before. One rolled through northern Europe between

2006 and 2009. In the UK, activists organised the first climate camps: tent cities serving as festivals of prefigurative living and learning and bases for mass action against some nearby point source of emissions – an airport, a coal-fired power plant, a financial district. A group called Plane Stupid occupied taxiways and leapt onto runways at airports around the country. In Denmark, Sweden and Germany, the fledgling movement went into high gear in the run-up to COP15 in Copenhagen, where a comprehensive agreement was expected to be negotiated; this time, we brought 100,000 people to the streets on a day-long march to the venue. Fifty thousand participated in the 'People's Climate Summit' in a sports and culture centre, several thousands in various blockades and other actions. It all yielded less than zero. COP15 ended with the delegates from the US and its allies killing the very idea of mandatory emissions cuts. Meanwhile, the onslaught of austerity policies in the wake of the financial crash claimed the energy of British activists, and so in 2009, following the debacle of COP15, the first twenty-first-century cycle came to a sharp end.

A second began in 2011, this time in the United States. After Barack Obama had failed to push through the promised cap-and-trade legislation at home and delivered the mortal blow to COP15, a frustrated movement left the halls of policy-making for the streets and launched a sustained campaign of civil disobedience. It focused on Keystone XL. A proposed pipeline for transporting oil from the Canadian tar sands to the refineries ringing the

Gulf Coast, the project required the approval of Obama, who was made to feel some 'people power': in August 2011, more than one thousand were arrested at a week-long sit-in outside the White House. Tens of thousands came back to encircle it with a human chain and lock themselves with plastic ties to its fences. At the same time, activists built a sprawling campaign for divestment, convincing universities, churches and other institutions with a minimum of conscience to sell off their stocks in oil, gas and coal companies so as to strip them of their legitimacy and prepare their downfall. Spurred on by Hurricane Sandy, New York City beat the record from Copenhagen with 400,000 people marching in the People's Climate March in September 2014, the largest rally until that date, and the tide seemed to be turning. The next year, Obama finally rejected Keystone XL. The last months of his presidency were marked by another high point of mobilisation, when Sioux nations drew supporters to a camp at Standing Rock in protest against the proposed Dakota Access Pipeline; as in the struggle against Keystone XL and dozens of other pipeline projects in North America, native activists took the lead of a movement that drew in tens of thousands of hitherto unpoliticised people. And then Donald Trump came to power. During his first week in the White House, he announced that both pipelines would be constructed at maximum speed, and the cycle came to a dead end.

But the crisis itself never relented. In the summer of 2018, a dome of heat lodged over the European continent, withheld the clouds for months on end and ignited firestorms of unseen intensity; in Sweden, military jets were called in to bomb the conflagrations (dropping not water bombs but actual explosives). The whole country seemed to shrivel. Towards the end of the summer, a fifteen-year-old girl, Greta Thunberg, took her bike to the Swedish parliament. She sat down on the pavement and declared a school strike for the climate. The picture of vulnerability and defiance – one lone adolescent girl, with a life on a warming planet ahead of her, against the stone-deaf walls of an entire political system – she touched a nerve in her generation. Children and youth began to walk out of their schools on Fridays. Waves of school strikes, known as 'Fridays for Future', rolled across western Europe and other parts of the world, reaching a first peak on 15 March 2019, when one and a half million struck and marched in what might have been the largest coordinated youth protest in history.

A few weeks later, Extinction Rebellion, or XR, another offspring of the hot summer of 2018, shut down much of central London as thousands of activists seized squares and bridges and slowly let themselves be dragged away by police. The largest civil disobedience action the UK had seen in decades, unfolding without a single incident of violence, placed XR at the crest of the third twenty-first-century cycle. Copies appeared on streets from New York to Sydney. XR had hit on a symbol as visually striking and easily replicable as the peace sign or the anarchist *A*: a stylised hourglass, representing the time running out, within a circle suggestive of the globe.

In early September 2019, I joined an XR action in my hometown of Malmö. The hourglass banners fluttered in the morning breeze from the sea, which, according to a newly released report, will drown much of the town later this century on current trajectories. Placards said 'Act now' and 'No more empty words'. Bands of activists marched between junctions and blocked them for a few minutes, while taking off their clothes and pretending to swim in the rising waters. Some soothed the irritation of the motorists by handing out snacks. In October – the waves of mobilisation now crashing against the walls with the regularity of an ocean – XR seized several junctions in central Berlin: some activists were dressed as penguins, tigers, bears; some juggled; some passed around vegan soup. But as I surveyed the scenes at Tiergarten and Potsdamer Platz, I realised that they bore little resemblance to the actions around COP1, merely by dint of the numbers. In politics, of course, numbers are everything. One worker staying home is a shirker, one thousand are a strike; one Greta is a girl in Stockholm, one million girls and boys a force to reckon with. The tents and picnics disrupting the flow of traffic in Berlin in late 2019 counted several thousands of participants, not hundreds; undergoing the most explosive growth, XR now claimed 485 affiliates across the world. The 'autumn uprising' began with the rising sun – as the Rebels of XR lyrically reported – in Sydney and moved on to European and North American cities, where the same hourglasses, slogans and disruptive actions moved into the spotlight in northern town centres, as though in a tightly choreo-graphed dance.

The growth curve continued as the Fridays for Future reached a new peak in late September 2019: now it was 4 million out one Friday, 2 million again the next, with protests registered in 4,500 locations on all continents including Antarctica (where climate researchers downed tools). The scales varied from one young woman in Minsk, Belarus, striking on her own to 50,000 children in school uniforms marching through Luanda, Angola. Students in the low-lying island nation of Kiribati chanted, 'We are not sinking, we are fighting.' But the epicentre of the mobilisation was Germany, home to more than one-third of all strikers in the world on 20 September, a fair share of them adults, some with the blessing of their unions.

In parts of the global North, the movement now appeared to make a qualitative leap into a mass phenom-enon. The cycle could well come to an inglorious end like the previous two, on account of an exogenous shock – a war in the Persian Gulf, a new financial crash – or missteps, but nothing indicated peak mobilisation just yet. There were potentials for continued growth, the cycle perhaps swinging into an even higher circuit, simply because the problem in itself followed that trajectory. It would not die away.

For the first time, the climate movement had become the single most dynamic social movement in the global

North, known for its youthful, joyful, exuberant, respect-
ful, orderly manifestations. But there was also a darker
undertone to the events: a simmering anger. Greta
Thunberg personified it. Her silhouette hovered above
millions of young people, as a sign of the intergenerational
injustice at the heart of climate breakdown. She was
mercilessly blunt when scolding world leaders for their
passivity. 'If the emissions have to stop, then we must stop
the emissions', she would say with incontestable, uncom-
promising logic, but 'no one is acting as if we were in a
crisis'. She went on a permanent tour through Fridays for
Future demonstrations, XR blockades, the beech and oak
groves of Hambach – a shred of an old-growth forest
surrounded by a brown coal mine in northern Germany,
whose owners wanted to tear it down – and the lawn of
the White House. In time for one more UN meeting on
climate in September 2019, she had reached the headquarters in New York, where her face nearly burst with
tears of rage: 'How dare you! You have stolen my dreams
and my childhood with your empty words. And yet I'm
one of the lucky ones. People are suffering. People are
dying', she said, excoriating her audience for still only
talking about money and economic growth and finishing
on a more than usually ominous note: 'Young people are
starting to understand your betrayal. The eyes of all future
generations are upon you. And if you choose to fail us I
say we will never forgive you' – 'change is coming, whether
you like it or not'. Some commentators noted the shift.
Back home in Sweden, one of them warned that if the

fences until they reach the open pits. There they slide down into the dusty craters and climb the diggers – the humungous excavators, like towering, rusty ships slowly eating their way through the earth – or lie down on the railway tracks ferrying coal to the furnaces. Production can be switched off for days. No fuel can be dug up and burnt when the activists hold the premises. Arguably constituting the most advanced stage of the climate struggle in Europe, Ende Gelände spanned the cycles and grew year on year; in the summer of 2019, 6,000 people closed the largest point source of emissions in Germany, backed up by several thousands more in the camp and some 40,000 in a Fridays for Future demonstration. By that time, Ende Gelände had forced the issue of brown coal to the top of the agenda and prompted a national commission to set a date for phasing it out – the date eventually announced as 2038. That's another two decades of churning out coal. Hence Ende Gelände promised to march on and swell further and spawn more copycats around Europe; in 2019, dozens of climate camps were organised from Poland to Portugal. The learning curve went steadily upwards.

Thus the cycles have not returned to square one, but rather formed a cumulative process and rising loop, like the climate crisis itself. The American and European sections have learnt from each other – divestment coming to English campuses, Greta Thunberg sailing to New York – and the cadres have accumulated a wealth of experiences. These include 'small wins' – a gas pipeline cancelled here, a coal plant scrapped there – as well as some big losses, which, however, seem to ensure the movement its growth, as the fire drives more people to take the plunge into activism. But so far, the movement has stopped short of one mode of action: offensive (or for that matter defensive) physical force. Anything that could be classified as violence has been studiously, scrupulously avoided. Indeed the commitment to absolute non-violence appears to have stiffened over the cycles, the internalisation of its ethos universal, the discipline remarkable.

One example: in late August 2018, some 700 activists assembled outside a compound of seven grey gas cisterns in the Dutch province of Groningen. Home to the largest onshore field of fossil gas in Europe, the area has long been racked by serial earthquakes, as the extraction has made the land suddenly compact and subside, damaging homes and buildings and racking the nerves of the local population. We erected an improvised camp in front of the compound, blocking transportation. The police lined up on a railway track between the gates and us. A ballast of crushed stones held up the rails. As dusk fell, some 300 farmers marched against Shell and Exxon and ended up in the camp, causing the crowd to spill onto the railway track, at which point the police started raining down their batons and shooting pepper spray, someone fainting and being carried away, others screaming in pain. Not a single stone was picked up and thrown. The supply was abundant – we were standing on top of thousands; we could have pelted them – and after such an assault, other types of crowds would have responded in kind. The climate movement would not.

The strictures against violence extend to property destruction. In Groningen, the 'action consensus' every participant had to abide by solemnly pledged that 'we will not damage machines or infrastructure'. A year later, the first Swedish imitation of Ende Gelände took place in Gothenburg against the construction of a gas terminal, one node in a fresh new infrastructure for fossil fuel combustion rolled out over the continent. A company called Swedegas engineered the terminal and aimed for eight more on the Swedish coast. Liquefied gas would be imported from across the world and pumped into the country through a network of pipelines, to the benefit of a global consortium of investors. And so we went there with our white coveralls, to the Gothenburg harbour, three fingers, 500 people – the largest civil disobedience action in the modern history of this somnolent nation – and blocked all trucks carrying oil and gas for a day. The action consensus stated that 'we will behave calmly and carefully'; further, 'it is not our aim to destroy or damage any infrastructure'. We spent the day sitting on the asphalt. Thus far, the movement for averting a spiralling climate catastrophe has not only been civil: it has been gentle and mild in the extreme.

There can be no doubt that this posture has served it well. It confers upon the movement a bundle of well-known tactical advantages. If it had deployed black bloc–like tactics from the start – donning sinister masks, smashing windows, burning barricades, fighting it out with the cops – it would never have attracted these numbers. The bar for joining a disruption of business-as-usual is lowered by certificates of peacefulness. Our being beaten up on the railway tracks in Groningen earned us the sympathy of the Dutch press; no one could smear us as terrorists or the like. Had some of us in Gothenburg started hacking on the fences or used slingshots against the trucks, the scene would have descended into chaos. We would have been kettled and herded off to jail; I could not have brought my two kids to the site and played with them for hours. Collective self-discipline – submitting to the guidelines of the operational leadership; conducting an action in accordance with plans – is a virtue. The determination of the movement to scale up its challenge to business-as-usual by means of ever bigger, bolder mass actions of precisely this kind cannot be called into question: this is the main way forward. Let a hundred Ende Gelände camps bloom and fossil capital might find itself under some real pressure.

What can be questioned, however, is something else. Will absolute non-violence be the *only* way, forever the sole admissible tactic in the struggle to abolish fossil fuels? Can we be sure that it will suffice against this enemy? Must we tie ourselves to its mast to reach a safer place? The question can be formulated in a different way. Imagine that the mass mobilisations of the third cycle become impossible to ignore. The ruling classes feel themselves under such heat – perhaps their hearts even melting somewhat at the sight of all these kids with handwritten placards – that their obduracy wanes. New politicians are voted into office, notably from green parties in Europe, who live up to their election promises. The pressure is kept up from below. Moratoriums on fresh fossil fuel infrastructure are instituted. Germany initiates immediate phase-out of coal production, the Netherlands likewise for gas, Norway for oil, the US for all of the above; legislation and planning are put in place for cutting emissions by at least 10 per cent per year; renewable energy and public transport are scaled up, plant-based diets promoted, blanket bans on fossil fuels prepared. The movement should be given the chance to see this scenario through.

But imagine a different scenario: a few years down the road, the kids of the Thunberg generation and the rest of us wake up one morning and realise that business-as-usual is still on, regardless of all the strikes, the science, the pleas, the millions with colourful outfits and banners – not beyond the realm of the thinkable. Imagine the greasy wheels roll as fast as ever. What do we do then? Do we say that we've done what we could, tried the means at our disposal and failed? Do we conclude that the only thing left is learning to die – a position already propounded by some – and slide down the side of the crater into three, four, eight degrees of warming? Or is there another phase, beyond peaceful protest?

Meanwhile in the actually existing capitalist world-economy, unfolding in parallel to the billowing climate movement, money flowed into the construction of fresh fireplaces. In May 2019, just weeks after the XR 'spring uprising' in London, the International Energy Agency (IEA) released its annual report on investment trends in the world of energy. Capitalists knew what sources to bank on. Two-thirds of capital placed in projects for generating energy in the year 2018 went to oil, gas and coal – that is, to *additional* facilities for extracting and combusting such fuels, on top of all that already spanned the globe – as against less than one-third of capital going to wind and sun. The share of renewables evinced no growth trend. In fact, global investment here edged downwards by 1 per cent (not a function of falling prices). Investment in coal, on the other hand, turned upwards for the first time since 2012, by 2 per cent – that is, investment in brand new coal supply not only continued but *increased*, although not as fast as in oil and gas. For the third consecutive year, the amount of money flowing into 'upstream' oil and gas, meaning infrastructure for delivering those fuels from under the ground, grew by 6 per cent – year on year, 6 per cent *more* capital was sunk into fresh drills, wells, rigs; investment in exploration alone was projected to shoot up by 18 per cent in 2019. The fire reignited itself anew.

The IEA saw glittering treasures ahead: ExxonMobil expected a profit in excess of 30 per cent from its novel deep-water fields off the coast of Brazil and Guyana. As ever, the financial picture for this line of business remained bright. The gas boom roared on, demanding 'new pipelines. Texas and the prolific Permian Basin is the epicentre of the development of new pipelines', but the steel snakes darted through the grass on other continents as well, their flammable breath about to reach, for instance, Sweden. Nowhere on the horizon of ongoing capital accumulation could a transition from fossil fuels to renewable energy be sighted (despite the latter now being 'consistently cheaper', as noted by the billionaire's rag *Forbes*). The IEA had tact enough to notice 'a growing mismatch between current trends and the paths to meeting' the goals of maximum 1.5°C or 2°C global warming. Put differently, the capitalist world-economy operated in fundamental disconnect from the sense and science of a planet on fire, not to speak of all aspirations to cool it down. And the disconnect was *widening*.

Timed for the XR 'autumn uprising', the *Guardian* published a series of revelations of just how much fossil capital prepares to burn. The world's fifty largest oil companies were poised to flood markets with more of their supply. Of that group, the two companies with the most aggressive plans were Shell and ExxonMobil, which planned for production to increase by 38 and 35 per cent, respectively, until 2030; on the second rung, BP foresaw a rise by 20 per cent, Total by 12. These circuits of accumulation were deeply intertwined with financial capital: as the *Guardian* also revealed, the three largest asset managers in the world, together handling assets worth more than China's entire GDP, continued to pour money into oil, gas and coal at an accelerating pace. Nothing could be more antithetical to the advice from the science or the needs of people and planet.

These trends were no flukes of the late 2010s. In the autumn of 2019, a team of scientists from California and Beijing headed by Dan Tong published an overview of the global investment landscape in *Nature* and began by duly repeating the official ambition to stay below 1.5°C or 2°C. 'Yet recent decades have witnessed an unprecedented expansion of historically long-lived, fossil-fuel-based energy infrastructure', they went on to gauge the mismatch – indeed, 'the youth of fossil-based generating units worldwide is striking', no less than 49 per cent of currently operating capacity having been commissioned *after* 2004, the year of COP10. Through its cycles so far, the climate movement has made no dent in these steadily spiralling curves. On the whole, it has not established physical contact with the adversary – primarily, of course, because the states standing in between have shielded fossil capital and punctiliously served it with everything needed for expanded reproduction. More than that: private capitalists and capitalist states are often impossible to tell apart, the latter behaving and investing just like the former.

Brick by brick, the fireplaces thereby build on themselves. Once an investor has constructed a coal-fired power plant or a pipeline or any other such unit, he will not want to dismantle it. Demolition on the morrow of completion would mean pecuniary disaster. It takes a lot of capital to get something like a deep-water field to pump up the black gold, and some time must pass before the initial investment pays off, and once profits have come gushing in, the owner will have an abiding interest in keeping the unit at work *for as long as possible*. Discarding it is not impossible; it would merely cause losses. It would liquidate capital. For this reason – economic, not technical – a unit of power generation from fossil fuels is expected to have a lifetime of around forty years. A plant or a pipeline built in 2020 should, from the standpoint of the investor, preferably still be in operation by 2060. Swedegas planned to pump gas into Sweden from the terminals under construction until that date. Coal-fired power plants often run even longer, for sixty years or more; the world's largest coal exporter, Australia, continues to open mines, notably the giant Adani mine in Queensland, to feed new-born plants in India and elsewhere, topped by a four-times-larger mine another company wants to build. The globe is wrapped in schemes of this kind. Thus scientists can calculate the 'committed emissions', defined as the CO_2 emissions to come if the infrastructure operates to the end of its expected lifetime. The more capital is ploughed into this field, the more emissions are committed (and the stronger the interest in defending business-as-usual, and the greater the mass of profit from fossil fuels, and the more money to reinvest . . .).

How much exactly? Tong and his colleagues estimated that committed emissions from already-running power plants – not counting extraction, transportation, deforestation – would be enough to take the world beyond 1.5°C. Combined with *proposed* plants, they would nearly exhaust the budget for the amount of carbon that can be released while still giving the world some chance of staying below 2°C. Another study from 2018 concluded that committed emissions from operating plants would surpass the limit for both temperature targets, while plants in various stages of the planning process would add the same amount as the extended commitment. Yet another found that incumbent and planned coal infrastructure alone would crash the 2°C budget. Something along these lines is, as the saying goes, in the pipeline.

How can capitalists go on like this? 'Current investments', the study on coal observes, can be seen 'as an indication that investors do not believe in future climate policy or that they are confident in their own lobbying power.' They still feel that they own the world. Fixed capital of this size is normally subject to risks and sensitive to the anticipated 'policy context'. Given the money involved, it would be imprudent to undertake these investments if swings and alterations in the economy threatened premature devaluation, let alone liquidation, but these capitalists do not see any wrecking balls coming their way. They think they have nothing to fear.

Many in the climate movement and most of its intellectuals would shudder at the thought of another stage beyond absolute non-violence, for a particular doctrine has taken hold: that of pacifism. It comes in two main forms. Moral pacifism says that it is always wrong to commit acts of violence. This has peculiar consequences. In August 2019, a young man appeared in a courtroom in the Norwegian capital of Oslo with thick purple bruises like ski glasses around his eyes, scratch marks all over his face, the wounds stretching down his neck: unmistakable signs of rough manhandling. The previous day, he had entered a mosque with two shotguns and a pistol and started shooting into the prayer room. Inspired by recent massacres at a mosque in Christchurch (fifty-one killed) and a shopping mall in El Paso (twenty-two killed), his intention was to kill the maximum number of worshippers – embodiments of the supposed threat to the white race – but barely had he fired his first bullets before a sixty-five-year-old man, Mohammed Rafiq, dressed in a *shalwar kameez* and sporting a big white beard, threw himself over the assailant. Rafiq knocked him to the ground, wrestled with him, warded off the young man's attempt to gouge out his eyes, kicked away his weapons and held him in a chokehold until the police arrived.

No massacre transpired. But evidently, Rafiq used a considerable amount of interpersonal violence in the encounter, which would imply his fall from pacifist grace: to a moral pacifist, Rafiq ought not to have resorted to such means. Moral pacifism claims to hold life in the highest regard and detest its violent termination, but a defensive act that saves lives and reduces violence is unacceptable to it insofar as it involves active physical force. This seems flawed. It also appears to yield a priori to the worst forms of evil: precisely those agents most intent on taking as many innocent lives as possible – fascist mass murderers, for instance – will be the least receptive to meek non-violent opposition. Indeed, the precepts of pacifism have often come across as exhortations to *surrender* to suffering and atrocity.

A moral pacifist can respond to this sort of objection by saying, 'Granted, some violence must be accepted in some cases' – at which point the pacifist, of course, ceases to be a pacifist and becomes like everyone else. Barring aforementioned fascists, very few believe that violence and war are inherent goods; almost all consider them prima facie bad things that can be justified only in certain cases, and then they proceed to disagree over what those cases are and what features they have in common. Among ethical standpoints, there is no such thing as 'contingent' or 'relative pacifism'. A pacifist who makes exceptions is a just war theorist. But there is another response available to the former: letting evil befall oneself without trying to strike it down has a value of its own. Moral pacifists have a way of inoculating themselves against mundane retorts such as 'what about your own child?' or 'what about the Second World War?' by retreating into a numinous place. Openly or vaguely, they valorise self-abnegation, crucifixion or some other sacrifice as held up by religious faith – or, to be precise, by a particular interpretation of some such faith. On this view, Mohammed Rafiq would have acted more virtuously had he remained seated on the floor when the murderer stormed in.

There are traces of moral pacifism in the teachings of Bill McKibben. The first cycle of the climate movement had no leader or figurehead, but the second had McKibben, a tireless organiser, an electrifying speaker, a prolific writer with more than a dozen book-length essays, a novel, an autobiography and countless stirring op-eds under his belt. Organic intellectual and conjurer of grassroots campaigns, he was a driving force behind the actions against Keystone XL, the movement for divestment and 350.org, the global network overlapping the second and third cycles. At the end of the former, he was dubbed 'the leading climate activist in the world'.

In McKibben's rendition of non-violence, 'there is a spiritual insight at its core'. That insight is 'the idea of turning the other cheek, of *taking on unearned suffering*', the latter a favourite trope of his, borrowed from Martin Luther King Jr. According to the adage from the reverend, 'unearned suffering is redemptive'. For someone who is not a disciple of this theology, the idea can be hard to grasp. Why would it be noble to subject oneself to suffering one doesn't deserve? The claim to oppose evil here appears to revert into a mystical rejoicing in it, as a sort of baptismal waterfall. More to the point: how can this be a premise for combatting the injustices of the climate catastrophe? If McKibben wanted to take on some unearned suffering, he could apply for citizenship in Dominica, set up a plantain and banana farm and wait for the next hurricane. If he wished the redemption of unearned suffering for others than himself – presumably the more generous attitude – then surely it would be most productive to let global heating run its course unopposed. McKibben obviously doesn't draw these conclusions, which speaks to his very great credit, but sacralisation of unearned suffering seems, at the least, an unstable plank for this struggle. Isn't suffering unearned by the victims precisely what is so morally repugnant about the unfolding crisis? If so, why make it a virtue?

Slipping out of the antinomies of moral pacifism, however, is the second version: the strategic one. It says that violence committed by social movements always takes them further from their goal. Turning to violent methods is not so much wrong as impolitic, ineffective, counterproductive – poor strategy, in short; non-violence is hallowed less as a virtue than as a superior means. Although derived from and accented by the moral source, it is this strategic doctrine that has gripped the imagination of the movement. McKibben now prefers to speak of non-violence in instrumental terms, as a 'technology' or 'technique', the greatest 'innovation' of the twentieth century; turning the other cheek is above all 'the tactically sound choice'. But it is XR that has codified the tenet most stringently. In its own origin story, the Rebellion began with a small group of people in the UK going to the library. Freaked out about unmitigated breakdown, they wanted to find a workable strategy for changing the behaviour of the powers that be, and what they found was 'the civil resistance model'. In the official handbook of the Rebellion, Roger Hallam, cofounder and ideologue, spells out the creed:

There are two types of disruption: violent and non-violent. Violence is a traditional method. It is brilliant at getting attention and creating chaos and disruption, but it is often disastrous when it comes to creating progressive change. Violence destroys democracy and the relationships with opponents which are vital to creating peaceful outcomes to social conflict. The social science is totally clear on this: violence does not optimize the chance of successful, progressive outcomes. In fact, it almost always leads to fascism and authoritarianism. The alternative, then, is non-violence.

Much as there is scientific consensus that global heating is the outcome of human deeds, so the sum total of social science and history – 'all the studies' – supply an unambiguous lesson: 'If you practise non-violence, you are more likely to succeed.' It follows that popular mobilisation against impending extinction 'has to stay non-violent. As soon as you allow violence into the mix, you destroy the diversity and community basis upon which all successful mass mobilizations are based.' Full compliance with this command is 'rule number one for all participants'. Rebels are instructed to offer flowers to the police. McKibben, for his part, frets about cracks in the discipline that might allow 'adventurers' to spoil the movement: only the purity and monopoly of non-violence gives it a fighting chance to win.

Such strategic pacifism is deduced from a particular reading not of faith, but of history. It has set the climate movement in the global North bubbling and fizzing with references to struggles past. One scholar has remarked on 'a whole new wave of comparisons' informing its vision, a surge in the interest in historical precedents – people winning against hopeless odds, great evil suddenly put to an end – that can break the hold of apathy. If they could prevail, the reasoning goes, so can we. If they changed the world by all means but violent ones, so we shall save it. Analogism has become a prime mode of argumentation and the main source of strategic thinking, most visibly in XR, the rare organisation that defines itself as a result of historical study. Note that the argument is not that violence would be bad at this particular moment – say, because the level of class struggle is so low in the global North that adventurist actions would only rebound and suppress it further: words that would never pass XR lips – nor that it might be expedient only under conditions of severe repression. Instead, analogist strategic pacifism holds that violence is bad in all settings, because this is what history shows. Success belongs to the peaceful.

The roster of historical analogies begins with slavery. If the abolitionists could turn the tables on that nefarious institution, so long taken for granted as a natural part of modern economies, through boycotts, mass meetings and thundering denunciations of iniquity, then we will do the same; just like us, they were first disparaged as crackpots and unreasonably impatient radicals, until righteousness gained the upper hand. Morals and strategy here blend. Abolition is conceived as a reprogramming of ethical codes – slavery went from foundation to abomination and fossil fuels will go the same way – and the abolitionists as armed with moral force. Or, as one Oxford professor much taken by XR and Greta Thunberg wrote in 2019, by way of analogy: 'The anti-slavery movement only took off once white people in Europe and America began to see people of African descent not as property but as people.'

Then there were the suffragettes. They obtained the vote for women through non-violent civil disobedience. XR has invoked them as role models; having shut down central London in April 2019, the Rebels earned themselves the sobriquet 'the new suffragettes'. One of the most avid arrestees, George Monbiot, recalled the suffragettes as an instructive example from the history researched by XR and applied 'to the greatest predicament humanity has ever faced'. Noblest and most cunning of all, however, was Gandhi. McKibben has revisited the history of the twentieth century and concluded that the mahatma is the one figure of that age who can still speak to us: 'I'm not sure I can think of a politics other than Gandhi's that offers much promise.' The mahatma not only drove the British from India but single-handedly launched the attack 'on the legitimacy of colonialism the world around', and if he could achieve all of this with his *ahimsa*, then we have a template for our times. Gandhi was the Einstein of non-violence, 'our scientist of the human spirit, our engineer of political courage'; McKibben has described how he returned from a trip to India early in the century with 'Gandhi on the brain' and rolled up his sleeves to tackle

back at what makes up the canon. Slavery was not abolished by conscientious white people gently disassembling the institution. The impulse to subvert it sprang, of course, from the enslaved Africans themselves, and they very rarely possessed the option of non-violent civil disobedience; staging a sit-in on the field or boycotting the food offered by the master could only hasten their death. From Nanny of the Maroons to Nat Turner, collective action against slavery perforce took on the character of violent resistance. The first sweeping emancipation of slaves occurred in the Haitian Revolution – hardly a bloodless affair. As some recall, slavery in the US was terminated by a civil war, whose death toll still remains close to the aggregate from all other military conflicts the country has been embroiled in. If there was one white abolitionist who helped precipitate that showdown, it was John Brown, with his armed raids on the plantations and armouries. 'Talk! Talk! Talk!' he exclaimed after yet another convention of a pacifist abolitionist society. 'That will never free the slaves! What is needed is action – action.'

Would slavery have ended without the slaves and their allies fighting back? The scholar who has most ambitiously sought to downplay the causal impact of slave revolts, Portuguese historian João Pedro Marques, has met with a barrage of criticisms from other specialists in the field. One of the most prominent, Robin Blackburn, has retorted that the very notion of slavery as unethical – harmful to the slaves, whom the masters wished to portray as happy and docile – originated in the acts of

explosive refusal. Even the most pacifist Quakers pointed
to the revolts as proof of the horrors of the peculiar institution. 'There was a cumulative character to anti-slavery
in the "age of abolition"', Blackburn writes: a steadily
rising tide of discontent and discomfort, sent off by the
quakes on the plantations. Granted, among a host of other
factors, the efforts of petitioners, demonstrators and legis-
lators contributed to the ending of slavery, but to reduce
the process to their efforts – or even to make them the gist
of the story – is about as accurate as the belief that yoga is
the sole path to human happiness.

The suffragettes are instructive. Their tactic of choice
was property destruction. Decades of patient pressure on
Parliament to give women the vote had yielded nothing,
and so in 1903, under the slogan 'Deeds not words', the
Women's Social and Political Union was founded. Five
years later, two WSPU members undertook the first militant action: breaking windowpanes in the prime minister's
residence. One of them told the police she would bring a
bomb the next time. Fed up with their own fruitless depu-
tations to Parliament, the suffragettes soon specialised in
'the argument of the broken pane', sending hundreds of
well-dressed women down streets to smash every window
they passed. In the most concentrated volley, in March
1912, Emmeline Pankhurst and her crews brought much
of central London to a standstill by shattering the fronts
of jewellers, silversmiths, Hamleys toy shop and dozens of
other businesses. They also torched letterboxes around the
capital. Shocked Londoners saw pillars filled with paper

throwing up flames, the work of some activist having thrown in a parcel soaked in kerosene and a lit match. The civil resistance model? More like the methods envisioned in Lanchester's paradox.

Militancy was at the core of suffragette identity: 'To be militant in some form, or other, is a moral obligation', Pankhurst lectured. 'It is a duty which every woman will owe her own conscience and self-respect, to women who are less fortunate than she is herself, and to all who are to come after her.' The latest full-body portrait of the movement, Diane Atkinson's *Rise Up, Women!*, gives an encyclopaedic listing of militant actions: suffragettes forcing the prime minister out of his car and dousing him with pepper, hurling a stone at the fanlight above Winston Churchill's door, setting upon statues and paintings with hammers and axes, planting bombs on sites along the routes of royal visits, fighting policemen with staves, charging against hostile politicians with dogwhips, breaking the windows in prison cells. Such deeds went hand in hand with mass mobilisation. The suffragettes put up mammoth rallies, ran their own presses, went on hunger strikes: deploying the gamut of non-violent *and* militant action.

After the hope of attaining the vote by constitutional means was dashed once more in early 1913, the movement switched gears. In a systematic campaign of arson, the suffragettes set fire to or blew up villas, tea pavilions, boathouses, hotels, haystacks, churches, post offices, aqueducts, theatres and a liberal range of other targets around the country. Over the course of a year and a half, the WSPU claimed responsibility for 337 such attacks. Few culprits were apprehended. Not a single life was lost; only empty buildings were set ablaze. The suffragettes took great pains to avoid injuring people. But they considered the situation urgent enough to justify incendiarism – votes for women, Pankhurst explained, were of such pressing importance that 'we had to discredit the Government and Parliament in the eyes of the world; we had to spoil English sports, hurt businesses, destroy valuable property, demoralise the world of society, shame the churches, upset the whole orderly conduct of life'. Some attacks probably went unclaimed. One historian suspects that the suffragettes were behind one of the most spectacular blazes of the period: a fire in a Tyneside coal wharf, in which the facilities for loading coal were completely gutted. They did, however, claim responsibility for the burning of motor cars and a steam yacht.

The incongruence of Gandhi has a different slant. Anyone who sees in him a paragon should pick up Kathryn Tidrick's masterful biography of the mahatma. During his time living in South Africa, he found his British masters marching off to the Boer War – and ran after, begging them to enlist him and his fellow Indians. A few years later, the British again paraded out to the provinces, now to the Zulus who rebelled against oppressive taxes and had to be flogged and mass executed into submission, and again Gandhi asked to serve. To his disappointment, he was taken on only as a stretcher-bearer and nurse on both occasions, but in his autobiography he claimed his share of martial glory by arguing that medical staff are as indispensable to war as any soldiers on the front. 'Gandhi famously resisted any use of violence', runs the standard characterisation, here in the words of yet another writer who thinks the climate movement should model itself on the mahatma. Did he? Perhaps the Boer and Zulu episodes were youthful blunders?

Hardly had the First World War broken out before Gandhi offered up to the Empire himself and as many Indians as he could dispose of. In early 1918, certain movements were busy trying to end the slaughter, agitating for soldiers to desert and turn against their generals, at which point Gandhi decided that more Indians had to be thrown into the trenches. 'If I became your recruiting agent-in-chief, I might rain men on you', he flattered the viceroy, promising another half million Indian men on top of the one million already in regiments or graveyards, leaving no stone in the countryside unturned in his search for eager volunteers (few showed up, which he considered a profoundly humiliating setback). In these recruitment drives, the mahatma pursued a logic of sorts. As long as Indians were effeminate and weak, the British would never consider them equals and grant them independence; to recuperate their manhood and strength, they had to become brothers-in-arms. Gandhi's strategy for national liberation never – this is true – condoned violence against the British, but it did include violence *with* them.

As for the former type, Gandhi mightily disapproved of the popular violence against the British occupation that seemed to accompany mass actions as surely as exhalation follows a deep breath. After setting up campaigns for *satyagraha*, engaging Indians in non-cooperation and lawbreaking en masse, he would receive word of crowds sabotaging transport systems, cutting telegraph wires, burning shops, breaking into police stations and attacking constabularies. He was flummoxed and livid every time. He likewise frowned upon anti-fascist resistance. In November 1938, in the days after Kristallnacht, the mahatma published an open letter to the Jews of Germany exhorting them to stick to the principles of non-violence and to delight in the results. 'Suffering voluntarily undergone will bring them an inner strength and joy.' In the case of war, Hitler might implement 'a general massacre of the Jews', but 'if the Jewish mind could be prepared for voluntary suffering, even the massacre I have imagined could be turned into a day of thanksgiving', for 'to the god-fearing, death has no terror. It is a joyful sleep'. Facing objections, Gandhi had to clarify his comments and add subsidiary arguments – Jews have never mastered the art of non-violence; if only they could take on their suffering with courage, even 'the stoniest German heart will melt' – indeed, 'I plead for more suffering and still more till the melting has become visible to the naked eye' (January 1939). In any case, 'the method of violence gives no greater guarantee than that of non-violence. It gives infinitely less.'

The pith of non-violence, in Gandhi's philosophy, was abstention from sexual intercourse: the soul would reach exalted heights only if it learned to 'crucify the flesh'. In the midst of mass mobilisation in 1920, he directed all Indians to go celibate until further notice. Best of all would be if humanity as a whole ceased to copulate; then the species would transmogrify into something holier. It followed that orphanages were unsound institutions, artificially keeping alive babies born out of excessive lust and thereby awarding unclean living. Hospitals had the same effect of 'propagating sin'. Disease, in the Gandhian view, results from impurity and must be allowed to do its cleansing work, and the same goes for extreme weather and earthquakes: with unusual consistency, the mahatma preached that victims of such events had it coming. 'Rain is a physical phenomenon; it is no doubt related to human happiness and unhappiness; if so, how could it fail to be related to his [*sic*] good and bad deeds?' One could descend considerably deeper into this rabbit hole.

Over his life, Gandhi's political compass gyrated wildly, the steady magnet being his view of himself as 'the pre-ordained and potentially divine world saviour', in Tidrick's summary. The fact that this man can emerge as an icon of the climate movement – not to mention 'our scientist of the human spirit' – attests to the depth of the regression in political consciousness between the twentieth and the twenty-first century. If the movement needs a lodestar from the past, it might as well choose the Sudanese Mahdi, Nostradamus, Rasputin or Sabbatai Zevi. Needless to say, the mass mobilisations led by the Indian National Congress had impressive features, and the Salt March and the withdrawal of cooperation with British authorities sent inspiration down the ages. But to attribute independence to them exclusively is, once again, to look at history with one eye. Subaltern violence marked the route to India, from the mutiny of 1857 to that of 1946; when the British finally packed up and left, a world war had intervened and drained the Empire of its strength: these were the years when decolonisation swept the globe. The selection of *satyagraha* as the take-away from that process serves only present wishes and biases. How did Algeria get free? Angola? Guinea-Bissau? Kenya? Vietnam? Ireland?

The civil rights movement is a better case for the pacifist argument. The Montgomery bus boycott, the lunch counter sit-ins, the Birmingham offensive, the Selma to Montgomery marches and other non-violent actions really did upend segregation in the South, showing African Americans a way to improve their lives and raising their consciousness to irreversible heights. As tactics for immediate gains and mass participation, they were far more effective than their reflexive detractors – among them Malcolm X – would allow. Indeed, so well did they work that some folks resolved to protect them with guns. In *This Nonviolent Stuff'll Get You Killed*, Charles E. Cobb Jr., himself a former field secretary for the Student Nonviolent Coordinating Committee (SNCC), tells the history of how the civil rights movement was girdled with armed protection. In the Deep South, rural African American communities had developed a long tradition of staving off murderous assaults with weapons; when the movement took root and began to deliver concrete benefits, it faced the same threat to physical survival. Klansmen and other white supremacists would surround movement bases in the night, assassinate activists, ambush marches and seek to drown the budding civil rights in blood. Too much was on the line for black communities to let that happen. Hence they produced stockpiled guns, refurbished movement bases – 'freedom houses' – into veritable fortifications, provided armed escorts for field secretaries from SNCC and CORE, organised armed caravans to and from mass meetings. Guns in hand, black people chased away Klansmen in the night, guarded picket lines from a distance, accompanied marches and voter registrations not in opposition to but *in unison* with the civil rights movement. Committed pacifists from the North tended to adapt to these realities. Even the reverend did: visiting Martin Luther King in his parsonage, soon after his home had been bombed, a journalist was about to sink into an armchair when he was alerted to a couple of loaded guns on it. 'Just for self-defence,' King explained.

'What is the best way to resist?' This was, in Cobb's account, the question African Americans asked themselves during the civil rights struggle. Non-violent civil disobedience caught on because it worked – better than the alternatives, such as guerrilla warfare against the state – and was appreciated precisely as a *tactic*, rather than as a creed or a doctrine. With such an approach to non-violence, deviations came naturally. The best way to resist in some circumstances (on a bridge patrolled by police) would not be the best in others (Klansmen encircling a house). 'From the beginning', Cobb affirms, 'the line between armed self-defense and the non-violent assertion of civil rights was blurred', and it was even more blurred in the wider picture.

The civil rights movement advanced through a spirited interplay with other African American currents. The burst of laws enacted to ensure the rights of black people in the 1960s was not entirely its own doing, the shared honour particularly evident for the Civil Rights Act of 1964, centrepiece of the new legislation. Why did the federal government meet the long-standing demands of Martin Luther King and his peers at this moment? The turning point came at the Birmingham offensive in 1963. When the sit-ins, kneel-ins and jail-ins against segregation in the city landed King in a prison cell, the first rocks and bottles flew. After two white supremacist bombings, the disturbances sped into the premier black urban riot of the era, with roving crowds assailing police officers and smashing property; for the first time, federal troops were sent in to quell such an eruption. From his cell, King could now signal a warning: if the demands of his movement were not met, other, more menacing forces would arise. If the channel of non-violence remained closed, 'millions of Negroes, out of frustration and despair, will seek solace and security in black nationalist ideologies' and then 'the streets of the South would be flowing with floods of blood'. Now *this* scenario curdled the blood of the Kennedy administration. Men who had the president's ear began to bombard him with the advice that unless major concessions were made, public order would break down. Absent swift results, 'Negroes unquestionably will look to untried and perhaps less responsible leaders' – notably Malcolm X – and before this spectre, the federal government acquiesced. The civil rights movement won the Act of 1964 *because it had a radical flank that made it appear as a lesser evil in the eyes of state power.*

That flank was associated with black violence, ever an incubus of the white American psyche. In the classical study of the radical flank effect, *Black Radicals and the Civil Rights Mainstream, 1954–1970*, Herbert H. Haines recaps the dialectic: 'Nonviolent direct action struck at the heart of powerful political interests because it could so easily turn to violence. The result was federal action designed to make further protest unnecessary.' And Birmingham, of course, was only the beginning: a few years later, the cities of the North were aflame – more than one thousand businesses damaged or destroyed in Newark alone in 1967; 313 riots nationwide in the first eight months of 1968 – and again the government tried to stem the tide by throwing fresh laws at the movement, such as the Civil Rights Act of 1968 banning racial discrimination in housing, passed amid the roar of sirens and crashing screens. Property destruction was a particularly distressing prospect. If the cities burned, 'the white man's companies will have to take the losses', whined one close adviser to Kennedy and Johnson. Over the course of the 1950s and '60s, the benchmark of moderation shifted rapidly, as the radicals of yesteryear – the civil rights leaders who incited people to break the law – came to look reasonable and restrained. Next to the threat of black revolution – Black Power, the Black Panther Party, black guerrilla groups – integration seemed a tolerable price to pay. Without Malcolm X, there might not have been a Martin Luther King (and vice versa).

The theory of the radical flank effect has application far beyond the African American struggle. The history of working-class politics in twentieth-century western Europe serves as an illustrative example. The vote, the eight-hour working day, the rudiments of a welfare state – the progress made by the reformist labour movement would have been inconceivable without the flank to the left and east of it. In the words of Verity Burgmann, 'the history of social movement activity suggests that reforms are more likely to be achieved when activists behave in extremist, even confrontational ways. Social movements rarely achieve everything they want, but they secure important partial victories' when one wing, flanking the rising tide in the mainstream, prepares to blow the status quo sky-high.

Now this provides food for thought to the climate movement. The fact that (as of this writing) it has not engendered a single riot or wave of property destruction would be taken as a sign of strength by the strategic pacifists, proof of correspondence with their ideal. But could it not also be seen as the opposite – as a failure to attain social depth, articulate the antagonisms that run through this crisis and, not the least, acquire a tactical asset? Does this movement possess a radical flank? Greta Thunberg might well be the climate equivalent of Rosa Parks, an inspiration she has acknowledged and often been compared to. But she is not (yet) an Angela Davis or a Stokely Carmichael.

Selective memory applies to South Africa too. It took more than divestment to bring down apartheid. It also took more than civil disobedience: in the 1950s and early '60s, the African National Congress (ANC) experimented with bus boycotts, strikes, pass-burning, campaigns to refuse segregation in trains and post offices and found that they invited little else than overwhelming repression. After the Sharpeville massacre in 1960, the ANC leaders realised that they had to ratchet up the pressure and formed Umkhonto we Sizwe, the Spear of the Nation, or MK. It was Nelson Mandela who pushed for the reorientation: 'Our policy to achieve a non-racial state by non-violence has achieved nothing', and so 'we will have to reconsider our tactics. In my mind we are closing a chapter on this question of a non-violent policy.' Having won over his colleagues to the new line, Mandela was appointed first commander of the MK.

> Our strategy was to make selective forays against military installations, power plants, telephone lines and transportation links; targets that would not only

hamper the military effectiveness of the state, but frighten National Party supporters, scare away foreign capital, and weaken the economy. This we hoped would bring the government to the bargaining table. Strict instructions were given to members of the MK that we would countenance no loss of life. But if sabotage did not produce the results we wanted, we were prepared to move on to the next stage: guerrilla warfare and terrorism.

Sabotage remained the main modus operandi of the MK. Rather like the suffragettes, the commando units crossing the borders into apartheid land struck against property – things like electric pylons and power stations. The actions had a rousing effect on the masses of the townships, who saw in them evidence that resistance was possible and streamed into the ANC. Songs, slogans, dances and other symbolic acts celebrating the MK suffused the mobilisation against apartheid into the 1980s, when the ANC captured its strategic doctrine in the formula of 'the hammer of armed struggle on the anvil of mass action'. There is not much for strategic pacifism to draw on here.

Reaching the days of Margaret Thatcher's poll tax, one must ask if there is a little censoring angel sitting on the shoulder of the strategic pacifist and instructing him in the ways of redaction. As everyone who has ever heard of the tax knows, the revolt culminated in mass riots in London that killed it off. That XR can devote an entire chapter to this struggle without mentioning this occurrence is indicative of the psychology of strategic pacifism: it is an exercise in active repression. None of the above is news or information hard to come by. The bloodletting in the slave revolts and the US civil war, the militancy of the suffragettes, Gandhi's devotion to the imperial army, the armed protection and radical flank of the civil rights movement, the Spear of the Nation – this is all in the public domain. And yet strategic pacifism adduces these sequences of struggle to admonish the climate movement against any aberration from non-violence. It is a mixture of cant and forgery. It reneges on its promise to treat civil disobedience as a tactic – something you do because it works well, which implies openness to reassessment. If non-violence is not to be treated as a holy covenant or rite, then one must adopt the explicitly anti-Gandhian position of Mandela: 'I called for non-violent protest for as long as it was effective', as 'a tactic that should be abandoned when it no longer worked.' Strategic pacifism turns this method into a fetish, outside of history, unrelated to time.

The logic of the comparisons would instead have to be inverted. It would need to say: admittedly, violence occurred in the struggle against slavery, against male monopoly on the vote, against British and other colonial occupations, against apartheid, against the poll tax, but *the struggle against fossil fuels is of a wholly different character and will succeed only on condition of utter peacefulness.* But would there be convincing reasons for such a position? Is the root system of fossil fuels within the prevailing order so shallow that they can be extracted with smaller effort than any of those other ills? Are they not entwined with overbearing power and fabulous profit? Should we expect there to be less friction, less conflict in *this* transition, in which emissions must go from ballooning to zero? Do our experiences so far tell us that we can accomplish this without ever having to contemplate other methods, or what exactly sets the climate apart from those other crises? If the analogies are taken seriously – and this emergency should indeed rank alongside slavery or apartheid – the conclusion would seem to tend towards the opposite. But in some respects, this emergency is worse.

It could be argued that humanity has never faced a situation like this before, and so comparisons with the past are void. There is some truth in this. The structure of the climate problem diverges from the analogues the movement likes to cite. Fossil fuel combustion is not a system for keeping a racially defined population in captivity and whipping the maximum amount of labour out of its bodies. One factor that made the Kennedy administration cave in to the civil rights movement was the embarrassment of cops brutalising demonstrators before rolling cameras, a prick in the moral superiority that the US claimed in the Cold War – a factor of a specific time, not to be conflated with the 2020s. Every conjuncture described above had concrete determinants not in place today. Most crucially, fossil fuels are not a political arrangement like limited franchise or pass laws: they and the technologies they power are *productive forces* imbricated in certain property relations. At this level of abstraction, the analogy with slavery does have some pertinence, as Maxine Burkett has suggested – enslaved people were also productive forces, used in a tremendously destructive fashion, embodying gigantic capital that had to be liquidated. Moreover, as climate scientist-cum-activist James Hansen has argued, fossil fuels, like slavery, cannot be the object of compromises; no one would consider reducing slavery by 40 per cent or 60 per cent. All of it must go.

Given that fossil fuels are this kind of thing, the toppling of dictators makes for poor parallels. Roger Hallam of XR holds up the image of thousands of demonstrators flowing into a square to demand the departure of a tyrant. 'The arrogance of the authorities leads them to overreact, and the people – approximately 1–3 per cent of the population is ideal – will rise up and bring down the regime. It's very quick: around one or two weeks on average. Bang: suddenly it's over. Unbelievable, but it happens that way.' Clearly it won't happen that way; fossil fuels will not be abolished in a week or two (nor was slavery). It won't conclude in miraculous fashion, because fossil fuels are not a rickety superstructure like the regime of Slobodan Milošević, swept away by the blow from people who aspire to basic freedoms shared by most everyone else. Business-as-usual is not a sideshow to bourgeois democracy, a relic from an authoritarian age that requires correction – it is the material form of contemporary capitalism, neither more nor less.

And yet the 'civil resistance model' is based on movements for ousting dictators, more precisely as they have been construed in *Why Civil Resistance Works* by Erica Chenoweth and Maria J. Stephan, the book the XR founders pored over in the library, a catechism of strategic pacifism. Chenoweth and Stephan place autocracy and foreign occupation in one corner and democracy and independence in the other. Then they classify campaigns for transitioning from the former to the latter as either violent or non-violent. Compiling more than 300 cases in a database, the bulk concerned with democracy, they conclude that non-violence is twice as likely to succeed. Palestinians went violent, Slovenians stayed non-violent; the former failed where the latter succeeded. The lesson for activists seems crystal clear, and is the source of the XR commandments.

Behind the sheen of arithmetic rigour, however, Chenoweth and Stephan exhibit the usual omissions and suppressions. They parade the campaign against Syrian presence in Lebanon in 2005 as an instance of non-violent triumph, but say nothing about the struggle by Hezbollah and other guerrillas to dislodge the incomparably more brutal and entrenched Israeli occupation; the fall of the Nepalese monarchy is ascribed to civil serenity, the Maoist insurgency left out; anti-apartheid is categorised as non-violent. Even non-violence against Hitler is depicted as more successful than violent resistance, a sleight of hand in true Gandhian spirit. This comparison of apples and oranges from history is designed to drive home the message that as soon as activists go violent, they cut their own throats, explaining disparate outcomes – why Slovenia is a democracy and Palestine is still occupied – and effectively turning activists into omnipotent agents in causal chains. The analogism drawn from Chenoweth and Stephan and turned into the XR model is not quite the intellectual bedrock.

On the other hand, it could be argued that while the climate crisis departs from all that came before it, we have no other experiences to fall back on than those gained in dissimilar struggles, such as against dictatorships. And long-lived autocracies can attain a rigidity and immutability reminiscent of the fossil economy. So we might look at one case of cardinal importance to Chenoweth and Stephan: Iran. They seek to establish the incompatibility between violence and mass mobilisation as a universal law, and the revolution that knocked down the Shah was indeed one of the most popular in history, directly engaging an estimated 10 per cent of the population – compared with, for example, the 1 per cent that participated in the overthrow of the Soviet Union. Incidentally, the run-up to the departure of the Shah had some elements reminiscent of recent climate mobilisations: demonstrations recurring at fixed intervals in the calendar, drawing ever-larger crowds; widening and intensifying strikes (including among oil workers); occupations of key sites (such as factories and palaces). What tipped the balance? In the story constructed by Chenoweth and Stephan, radical Iranians first sought to defeat the Shah by means of armed struggle in the 1970s, notably through the Marxist guerrilla group known as the Fedaiyan, and failed dismally. But when they switched to non-violence, they reached their goal in no time.

The problem is that this sounds, once again, more like a morning prayer than an account of what happened. The most detailed extant chronicle of the process, Misagh Parsa's *Social Origins of the Iranian Revolution*, delineates a torrent of popular onslaughts rising so high as to eventually submerge the Shah regime, from Mazandaran in the north to Mashhad in the east. Having sustained attacks from the army, government thugs, the civil police and the secret police known as SAVAK for months, the mobilised masses 'aggressively struck back at the armed forces' in the autumn of 1978. In Amol, they equipped themselves with bows and poisoned arrows, overwhelmed the garrisons and seized their weapons; in Dezful, they dropped bags of sand on patrolling soldiers, who were then jumped upon and disarmed; in Hamadan, they burnt down government buildings until the city 'came to resemble an ancient ruin'; in the capital Tehran, hundreds of such buildings and banks were on fire by early November. In Ahvaz, managers of US oil companies were shot or had their cars set alight. From Kermanshah in the west to Kerman in the south, furious crowds laid siege to SAVAK offices, tore down statues of the Shah, stormed the homes of regime officials, took over cities and defended them against thugs;

having stocked up on arms plucked from the enemy, the revolutionaries formed myriad militias. The Fedaiyan rushed forth and pounced upon police stations, military trucks, gendarmeries. But 'most of the violence of the crowds was directed at property, not at people'. All of this surged higher and higher *in tandem* with a general strike crippling production and mass demonstrations – several millions on the march by December – paralysing the streets. By February 1979, a situation of dual power had emerged, with remnants of the regime clinging onto power through the military. At that point, commandos from the Fedaiyan joined mutinous air force cadets and 'broke the deadlock through an armed insurrection', in the words of Asef Bayat, preeminent scholar of the Iranian Revolution. It was at this point the forces of the Shah were routed. A moment of mass euphoria supervened.

Some chapters from this story were re-scripted for Tahrir Square, which, since the eighteen days in the spring of 2011, has entered strategic-pacifist lore as one more proof of peace power. But the millions of Egyptians did not reach that square by offering flowers to the police. On the decisive Friday of Anger, 28 January, they picked up gas canisters, pieces of pavements and other projectiles and fought their way through the dense cordons across the bridges to Tahrir – 'a confrontation that turned peaceful protesters into violent protesters who defeated the riot police out of necessity and despair', to quote M. Cherif Bassiouni's hefty *Chronicle of the Egyptian Revolution and Its Aftermath*. Of the eighteen days it took to expel

Mubarak, the three first might possibly count as non-violent. During the remainder, at least one-fourth of the country's police stations – over 50 per cent in Cairo, over 60 in Alexandria – were sacked. The national tally of demolished police vehicles reached 4,000. The effect of this detonation of mass violence against the police (which, needless to say, was responsible for the vast majority of the casualties) was not to scare away ordinary people, but precisely the contrary: it invited them to Tahrir. It opened the sluice-gates across the Nile, by burning policemen out of their stations and degrading the repressive capacity of the state to such an extent that it could only look on as the demonstrators took over. Contravening 'the civil resistance model', anti-regime violence and street protests were '*synergetic and complementary*', in the words of Neil Ketchley, another student of the Egyptian Revolution. And this seems more like the rule than the exception.

Indeed, Ketchley and his colleague Mohammad Ali Kadivar have sifted through all democratic transitions that occurred between 1980 and 2010 and found that as a rule, dictators are unseated by people who first come in peace and then, after running into the iron-clad state, swing sticks, throw stones and hurl Molotov cocktails. They call this 'unarmed collective violence'. Practised by civilians, improvised weapons in hand, this is not violence exercised by a standing army with high-tech weaponry. But it can be flung against the repressive state apparatus and dispensed against property to smashing effect: it 'disrupts the civic order and so raises the costs of ruling for an incumbent regime'. Unarmed collective violence was present in the lion's share of the transitions, but ignored by Chenoweth and Stephan, who had to exorcise it to generate their result, their 'twice as likely' conclusion hiding the mad multitudes from Chile to Indonesia, Pakistan to Madagascar, even Serbia. Other scholars have contributed to the debunking of their data set. Chenoweth and Stephan are not the IPCC of resistance.

The remaining question is whether it is possible to locate *even one minimally relevant analogue to the climate struggle that has not contained some violence.* Strategic pacifism is sanitised history, bereft of realistic appraisals of what has happened and what hasn't, what has worked and what has gone wrong: it is a guide of scant use for a movement with mighty obstacles. The insistence on sweeping militancy under the rug of civility – now dominant not only in the climate movement, but in most Anglo-American thinking and theorising about social movements – is itself a symptom of one of the deepest gaps between the present and all that happened from the Haitian Revolution to the poll tax riots: the demise of revolutionary politics. It barely exists any longer as a living praxis in powerful movements or as a foil against which their demands can be set. From the years around 1789 to those around 1989, revolutionary politics maintained actuality and dynamic potentiality, but since the 1980s it has been defamed, antiquated, unlearned and turned unreal. With the consequent deskilling of movements comes the reluctance to recognise revolutionary violence as an integral component. This is the impasse in which the climate movement finds itself: the historical victory of capital and the ruination of the planet are one and the same thing. To break out of it, we have to learn how to fight all over again, in what might be the most unpropitious moment so far in the history of human habitation on this planet.

And here we reach the one dimension that most distinctly sets this crisis apart: time. When the suffragettes took to the streets, they had had enough of women being excluded from the state for centuries. From his Birmingham jail, Martin Luther King pointed out that 'we have waited for more than 340 years for our constitutional and God-given rights' and explained to his white addressees that 'there comes a time when the cup of endurance runs over'. Many if not most struggles in the past have obeyed such a temporality of exasperation – enough is enough, *¡Ya basta!*, etc. – but in this case, it is subordinate to prognostication. The worst has not happened; it is on the way, at speed. Perhaps an applicable analogy here is with fascism (the resistance against it ever the worst case for pacifists). In the early 1930s, it became more evident by the month that Germany was slipping down a slope that would end in the Nazi seizure of power. 'How much valuable, irretrievable time has been lost! As a matter of fact, not much time is left,' cried one of the voices that most insistently warned of the danger and urged his audiences to spare no efforts in combatting it (here in December 1931). Now one shouldn't exaggerate the contrast between these two lines of time – they cross each other: the emergency is already here, the cup of endurance fast running over – but the onrush of catastrophe does have a temporality of its own. It imposes tight constraints on those who want to fight.

2

Breaking the Spell

At the time of COP1, few would have thought that two or three decades down the line, the economies of the world would discharge nearly one gigaton of carbon per month, the corporations busily planning for augmented capacity to combust fossil fuels and the governments presiding over it all, proudly or passively. The irresponsiveness to the crisis has exceeded expectations. So has, no less fatefully, the response of the climate system: at the time of COP1, few scientists foresaw that the land and the oceans so soon would fail to soak up the gases emitted, become overfilled and disturbed and start leaking and puffing carbon dioxide and methane at such a rate. The northern zone of permafrost, for instance, is a subterranean storehouse of carbon frozen for hundreds of thousands of years. When the planet heats up, the soil begins to thaw, microbes set to work on the organic matter and decompose it, releasing carbon dioxide but mainly methane – a greenhouse gas with eighty-seven times greater warming effect during the first two decades in the atmosphere – a process now accelerating beyond the predictions. Forest fires work the same way. Carbon locked into trees and soil escape when the flames pass through, as they now do more often, for longer periods, at higher intensity, over vaster territories, the primary fires of fossil fuels igniting secondary fires from Kamchatka to the Congo. Scientists lag behind these positive feedback mechanisms and struggle to capture them in their models. The carbon budgets have yet to fully integrate them, and if they would, they would contract further: if the thawing permafrost and proliferating wildfires and other mechanisms were accounted for, there would be *even less* of a margin available to stay below 1.5°C or 2°C.

Thus we find ourselves between two scissor blades: on the one hand, unbending business-as-usual, taking emissions ever higher and confounding hopes for mitigation; on the other, delicate ecosystems crashing down – the extraordinary inertia of the capitalist mode of production meeting the reactivity of the earth. This is the temporal predicament in which the climate movement has to devise meaningful strategies. 'Even under optimistic assumptions', the pathways to a 'tolerable future' are 'rapidly narrowing', in the words of the umpteenth scientific supplication for 'immediate global action'. Using models with incomplete representation of positive feedback mechanisms, writing in 2019 – another year of rising emissions – Dan Tong and his colleagues concluded that

1.5°C still remained 'technically possible' on two conditions. First, to have 'a reasonable chance' of respecting the
limit, human societies would have to institute '*a global
prohibition of all new CO_2-emitting devices*'. Now the likelihood of the ruling classes implementing a global prohibition of all new CO_2-emitting devices because scientists
tell them to, or because billions of people would otherwise
suffer grievous harm, or because the planet could spin
into a hothouse, is about the same as them lining up at the
summit of the steepest mountain and meekly proceeding
to throw themselves off the edge.

So here is what this movement of millions should do,
for a start: announce and enforce the prohibition. Damage
and destroy new CO_2-emitting devices. Put them out of
commission, pick them apart, demolish them, burn them,
blow them up. Let the capitalists who keep on investing in
the fire know that their properties will be trashed. 'We are
the investment risk', runs a slogan from Ende Gelände,
but the risk clearly needs to be higher than one or two
days of interrupted production per year. 'If we can't get a
serious carbon tax from a corrupted Congress, we can
impose a de facto one with our bodies,' Bill McKibben has
argued, but a carbon tax is so 2004. If we can't get a prohibition, we can impose a de facto one with our bodies and
any other means necessary.

That, however, would only be a start, for the second
condition for staying below 1.5°C – or indeed any other
boundary between a tolerable and an intolerable future
– would be 'substantial reductions in the historical

lifetimes' of fossil fuel infrastructure. Not only new but existing, young and old CO_2-emitting devices would have to be deactivated. The science is eminently clear on this point. Because so much valuable, irretrievable time has been lost – as a matter of fact, not much time is left – assets have to be stranded. Investments must be written off too early for capitalist taste; on one estimate, the instant suspension of every project in the pipeline would make 2°C achievable only if accompanied by the decommissioning of one-fifth of all power plants running on fossil fuels (this estimate is as of 2018 – more years or decades of business-as-usual would raise the requirement). That is a lot of already sunk capital. Now one reason why climate stabilisation appears such a frightfully daunting challenge is that no state seems prepared to even float this idea, because capitalist property has the status of the ultimate sacred realm. Who dares to throw it on the scrapheap? What government is willing to send in its forces to ensure the forfeiture of this amount of profit? And so there must be someone who breaks the spell: 'Sabotage', writes R. H. Lossin, one of the finest contemporary scholars in the field, 'is a sort of prefigurative, if temporary, seizure of property. It is' – in reference to the climate emergency – 'both a logical, justifiable and effective form of resistance and a direct affront to the sanctity of capitalist ownership.' A refinery deprived of electricity, a digger in pieces: the stranding of assets is possible, after all. Property does not stand above the earth; there is no technical or natural or divine law that makes it inviolable in this emergency. If states cannot on their own initiative open up the fences, others will have to do it for them. Or property will cost us the earth.

The immediate purpose of such a campaign against CO_2-emitting property, then, would be twofold: establishing a disincentive to invest in more of it and demonstrating that it can be put out of business. The first would not require that all new devices be disabled or dismantled, only enough to credibly communicate the risk. Strict selectivity would need to be observed. There was a randomness to the property destruction undertaken by the suffragettes, which wouldn't do now; if activists from the climate movement were to attack post offices and tea shops and theatres, investors would not be dissuaded from anything in particular. It would have to be coal wharfs and steam yachts only this time. But just as the suffragettes sought to twist the arm of the state – on their own, they could not legislate any voting rights – the aim would be to force states to proclaim the prohibition and begin retiring the stock. 'The current global energy system is the largest network of infrastructure ever built, reflecting tens of trillions of dollars of assets and two centuries of technological evolution', 80 per cent of which energy still comes from fossil fuels. No one in his or her right mind would think that bands of activists could burn all or one fifth of that to the ground (or that such a tertiary fire would be unequivocally desirable). At the end of the day, it will be states that ram through the transition or no one will.

But the states have fully proven that they will not be the prime movers. The question is not if sabotage from a militant wing of the climate movement will solve the crisis on its own – clearly a pipe dream – but if the disruptive commotion necessary for shaking business-as-usual out of the ruts *can come about without it*. It would seem fool-hardy to trust in its absence and stick to tactics for normal times. Recognising the direness of the situation, it is high time for the movement to more decisively shift from protest to resistance: 'Protest is when I say I don't like this. Resistance is when I put an end to what I don't like. Protest is when I say I refuse to go along with this anymore. Resistance is when I make sure everybody else stops going along too', as one West German columnist wrote in 1968, relaying the words of a visiting Black Power activist. There will be no shortage of objections to such resistance. Would it, to begin with, be technically possible?

'Pipelines are very easily sabotaged. A simple explosive device can put a critical section of pipeline out of opera-tion for weeks', the *Pipeline and Gas Journal* lamented in February 2005. At that point, the Iraqi resistance against US occupation had executed nearly 200 attacks on pipe-lines. 'The sabotage campaign has created an inhospitable investment climate and scared away oil companies that were supposed to develop its oil and gas industry', the *Journal* snivelled; to make matters worse, similar offences were committed in the part of Kurdistan under Turkish control and in Chechnya, Assam and Colombia, where leftist guerrillas had pierced a key pipeline so frequently that 'it became known as "the flute"'.

There is a long and venerable tradition of sabotaging fossil fuel infrastructure, for other reasons than its impact on the climate. The ANC considered oil supply an Achilles' heel of apartheid. In the 1960s, the white state set up the company Sasol to ensure its energetic foundation, not the least by converting abundant domestic coal to synthetic petroleum through hydrogenation, a chemical process much advanced by the Nazis. One of the most spectacular actions in the freedom struggle targeted Sasol. In June 1980, commando units from MK cut holes in the security fences around two hydrogenation facilities and planted mines in their tanks. Lasting for three days, the smoke plume could be seen by electrified audiences in Johannesburg: it 'shattered the myth of white invulnerability. It was not about the quantity of oil that was lost . . . it was that column of smoke that was important. Sasol was a symbol of power,' in the words of ANC militant Frene Ginwala. In the assessment of Mandela, the action contributed to the revival of the movement in the early 1980s. 'None of these attacks', one scholar of the MK asserts, 'came close to bringing down the state, but they provided physical evidence of a tangible *potential* threat to the regime – reinforcing the sense, as Nadine Gordimer put it, that "something out there" represented a shadowy threat to the long-term future of white supremacy.' The façade of durability had been fractured.

But the pioneer of pipeline sabotage is the Palestinian resistance. In the wake of the First World War, European and American oil companies swooped down on the depots discovered in the Persian Gulf. For the British Mandate in Palestine, the central industrial project became the construction of a pipeline, cutting straight from Kirkuk across the Jordanian desert into the northern West Bank and Galilee and all the way to the refinery in Haifa, from which Iraqi oil could be delivered to the world market. When the Palestinians rose in a general strike in 1936 – the most formidable anti-colonial uprising of the era – much of the action came to revolve around the pipeline. Two months after the strike commenced, rebels blasted it for the first time. At the zenith of the three-years-long revolt, they tore it apart almost every night: set it ablaze or punctured it with pot-shots; along the sections where it was buried underground, bands of five or six would dig into the soil, expose the pipe, break it and throw in flaming rags wrapped around stones. Forced to close the line again and again, the British colonisers were deprived of their main source of revenue and energy. As it stretched unguarded over long distances, they were 'unable to defend this vital pipeline, and admitted so much', in the words of Ghassan Kanafani, the wordsmith of the Popular Front for the Liberation of Palestine (PFLP), while 'the "pipe" as the Palestinian Arab peasants called it was enshrined in the folklore which glorified acts of popular heroism'.

Sabotage along the same lines was relaunched by the PFLP in 1969. In May of that year, six fighters from the Front sneaked into Israeli-occupied territory from southern Lebanon, trekked across the mountainous terrain of the Golan Heights and located an unguarded portion of the pipeline carrying crude oil from Saudi Arabia to the Mediterranean. They stayed overnight, excavated the pipeline, planted an explosive device and slipped away. Weeks later, another cell infiltrated the refinery in Haifa and set off a bomb, and before the end of the summer, the PFLP had also demolished two high-voltage towers and a pipeline in the Naqab desert. *Al-Hadaf*, the weekly newspaper of the PFLP edited by Kanafani, explained that the aim was to 'hit the enemy economically, specifically in the frame of oil production'. In a recent reconstruction of the campaign of 1969, Zachary Davis Cuyler has shown that the Front understood oil as a material base for the hostile trinity – US imperialism, Israeli colonialism, Arab reaction – and sabotage as a way to 'strike at the ligaments of empire'.

In the time of the *Pipeline and Gas Journal* lament, however, it was Nigeria that saw the most extensive property destruction. After the non-violent movement against the oil corporations ravaging the Niger Delta appeared to have hit a brick wall in the late 1990s, the organised youth of Ijaw and other communities made a bid to eject them by force. In late 2005, the Movement for the Emancipation of the Niger Delta (MEND) announced itself by giving these corporations the ultimatum to leave or 'face violent attacks'. Inaugurating a guerrilla war unique for its concentration on oil, MEND then undertook 'a fantastically audacious series of attacks', with Michael Watts: moving swiftly on boats through the creeks and swamps to blow up pipelines, strike vessels, overpower offshore platforms, assault offices, kidnap oil employees. The first in the series was labelled 'Operation Cyclone'. Between 2006 and 2008, when the insurgency stood at its height, MEND shut down a third of production in Africa's principal oil country. 'The stable and regularised flow of oil', Watts observed, 'was placed in question in an historically unprecedented way.' For a brief moment, it seemed as though Shell, ExxonMobil and the other predators were on the verge of withdrawal.

During the Egyptian Revolution, the pipeline the Mubarak regime used to supply the state of Israel with gas – below market prices – attracted some of the popular rage. After ten sabotage actions closed the spigots, Israel cancelled payments and the agreement broke down. An estimated thirty explosions rocked the pipeline in the period between the eighteen days of protest that brought down Mubarak and the coup of Abdel Fattah al-Sisi. In India, the Naxalites have struck regularly against coal mines and railways; in 2009 and 2010, authorities complained that they strangled transportation of the fuel and established de facto no-go zones for investors wishing to open new mines, shaving off one-fourth of the country's coal output. Among other actions in the summer of 2019, Naxalites attacked coal transports in the state of Chhattisgarh, set ablaze sixteen vehicles carrying coal in Jharkhand and torched twenty-seven machines and vehicles at a construction site for a national highway in Maharashtra plus a coal tar plant, with no end in sight.

The Egyptian and Indian revolutionaries had little in common, but fossil fuel infrastructure was targeted by both.

Then a new record was set in the Gulf. None of the above came close to the effect of the drones launched by the Houthi rebels in Yemen – another country with a tradition of pipeline sabotage – against Aramco's refineries in Abqaiq, the world's biggest oil processing facility, on 14 September 2019. The unmanned vehicles swarmed into the precincts to puncture storage tanks, light fires, disable processing trains; in one fell stroke, half of the oil production in Saudi Arabia, accounting for 7 per cent of global supplies, had to be taken offline. No single action in the history of sabotage and guerrilla war had achieved a commensurate break on the pumping of oil. According to a chorus of pundits, it heralded a new era of asymmetric warfare: now rebels can use tiny, cheap, toy-like planes to knock out pillars of the energy system. Business news site Bloomberg quivered. The Abqaiq action provided 'stark evidence of the vulnerability of global crude supply in an age of disruptive technologies that can bring a century-old industry to its knees – at least temporarily'. What more could a climate activist dream of?

Given this record from the past and present, the question is not whether it's technically possible for people organised outside of the state to destroy the kind of property that destroys the planet; it evidently is, just as it's technically possible to shift to renewable energy. The question is *why these things don't happen* – or rather, why they happen for all sorts of reasons good and bad, but not for the climate. It is Lanchester's paradox in the global South. Commodities that combust fossil fuels may be comparatively thinly spread in the South, but it is sufficiently crisscrossed by infrastructure for their *production* to be home to the richest tradition of sabotage. The South reels under the blows from climate breakdown. It has the most to lose in the short and medium term, and popular concern is rife, far higher than in the North, according to some polls. This is where the know-how of grand property destruction is most alive, and still it is conspicuous by its absence. Two explanatory factors spring to mind: the general demise of revolutionary politics, steeper for the higher point of departure in the South than in the North, bringing down the levels of consciousness required to connect the dots, and, more particularly, insufficient politicisation of the climate crisis. People might agonise over it; they rarely see a means for fighting back.

Consider the country of Egypt. It is extremely vulnerable – the rising sea penetrating the Delta and spoiling fields with salt water; the summer heat growing insufferable in Cairo; the harvests in Upper Egypt predicted to shrink faster than in most other breadbaskets; the rates of evaporation in Lake Aswan and the Nile poised to spike – and yet the climate question is all but dead. Right after the fall of Mubarak, there was a tiny opening for popular engagement with it. Then Sisi brought down the curtain and turned the country sharply towards more fossil fuels. Not only did he revamp and reverse the agreement with

Israel – now it would be Egypt importing newly discovered gas from territories controlled by that state – he also made a dash for coal, planning for an eightfold increase in combustion capacity, overseeing construction of the largest coal-fired power plant in Africa (if not, as the Chinese-Egyptian conglomerate claimed, in the world). Initial protests were snuffed out, an unhappy environmental minister sacked. Few countries have seen a similar recent spurt in the growth of committed emissions. Few are so blessed with sunlight and wind that are so egregiously unexploited (accounting for less than 1 per cent of electricity generation under Sisi). Few combine these factor endowments with an equally fresh and raw history of revolutionary struggles that includes sabotage – but those struggles have been utterly squashed. Perhaps one day, millions of Egyptians will stream into the zone of the Suez Canal to protest against the forces wrecking their lives and some of them veer off towards Sisi's coal plants; perhaps that could make a difference. But that day is too distant for comfort.

There are comparable compounds in other countries of the global South. Iran lurches from one climate disaster to the next, has a ruling class of millionaire mullahs sitting on riches from oil and gas, leaves potentials for renewable energy untapped and boasts a sprawling tree of revolutionary politics, razed in the years after 1979. The Fedaiyan is no more. South Africa, Nigeria, Colombia and many others fit the broad pattern. But sabotage of fossil fuel infrastructure is not patented by the global South; in fact, it is as old as the infrastructure itself, going back to the Luddites and the Plug Plot Riots and other working-class movements taking it out on steam-engines and industrial machines in England, which only makes the paradox more mysterious. Devices emitting CO_2 have been physically disrupted for two centuries by subaltern groups indignant at the powers they have animated – automation, apartheid, occupation – but not yet as destructive forces *in and of themselves.*

Western Europe had its own moment of sabotage in the 1970s and '80s, in solidarity with the liberation struggles in what was then known as the Third World. In 1972, Palestinian militants blasted a pipeline belonging to Esso – now ExxonMobil – near Hamburg. In the mid-1980s, cadres from the 'anti-imperialist front' – Action Directe (France), Rote Armee Fraktion (Germany), Cellules Communistes Combattantes (Belgium) – teamed up for a campaign against NATO pipelines traversing their countries; a dozen pipes and pumping stations were blown up. As part of the international outcry against apartheid in the 1980s, activists firebombed petrol stations of companies that continued to trade with South Africa, notably Shell stations in the Dutch province of Groningen. Shell stations were occupied and burnt out in Sweden in the mid-1990s in revulsion against the treatment of the peoples of the Niger Delta. But for the climate, nothing of the sort.

One facet of the retrogression in Europe in recent years is the far right's virtual monopolisation of political

violence, the France of Gilets Jaunes being the main exception. During the so-called refugee crisis of 2015, ninety-
two arsons were committed against asylum centres in
Germany – a mirroring of the radical flank effect, on the
farthest right – pushing the state towards closed borders; a
similar spate of fires coursed through Sweden, the second
main recipient of migrants in the EU. Not a single attack
was registered against fossil fuel infrastructure in either
country. That distribution must fall under the headline of
pathological human irrationality in the midst of this crisis.
Property destruction still happens – it's just done by the
wrong people for very wrong causes. But it doesn't have to
come in the form of explosions, projectiles, pyromania; it
doesn't presuppose the military capabilities of the PFLP,
the MEND or the Houthis. It can be performed without
a column of smoke. That is preferable. Sabotage can be
done softly, even gingerly.

On a warm, quiet night in July 2007, Östermalm, the
most affluent neighbourhood in central Stockholm, home
to billionaires and aristocrats and an ambience of stately
calm, received a visit from a group of young women and
men who lived elsewhere in the city. Someone took her
dog for a night walk. Someone peered out the window
before turning off the light. Someone wobbled home on
his bike, but no one seemed to notice us when we walked
up the streets, stopped and bent down, walked again at a
fast clip, stopped and bent down, rose, moved on. Along
the sidewalks of Östermalm, the trail of a hissing, fizzling

sound unfolded for hours. In the morning, sixty owners of SUVs found their cars reclining on the asphalt. On their windscreens, they had a leaflet to read:

> We have deflated one or more of the tyres on your SUV. Don't take it personally. It's your SUV we dislike. You are certainly aware of how much gas it guzzles, so we don't need to enlighten you about it. But what you seem to not know, or not care about, is that all the gasoline you burn to drive your SUV on the city's streets has devastating consequences for others,

and then we recited the ABC of the crisis. We pointed out that as an affluent Swede, the owner would be fine for some time – unlike poor people far away, those first to be pummelled by the storm. The worst of that storm could still be averted 'if we slash emissions. Now. Not tomorrow. That's why we have disarmed your SUV by releasing the air from the tyres. Since you live in a city with decent public transport, you will have no difficulty getting to your destination. / Asfaltsdjungelns Indianer', the signature line translating to 'Indians of the Concrete Jungle', admittedly a silly and even inappropriate name. (We received an email from a Native American upset about our cultural appropriation.) In the wee hours, we claimed responsibility for this first action in a communiqué to the press and launched a blog. There we enjoined others to get to work.

The blog contained a list of images and names of the main SUV models – from the Volvo XC90, the best-selling specimen in Sweden at that point, to the notorious Hummer – and a simple manual. Unscrew the cap on the valve of the tyre. Inside, there is a pin that will release the air if pushed down. Insert a piece of gravel the size of a boiled couscous grain or corn of black pepper – or, we suggested, use a mung bean – and screw the cap back on. With the little object pressing down the pin inside the valve, the tyre will be fully deflated after about an hour. Don't forget to stick the printable leaflet under the windscreen wiper, so the owner can't miss the tinkering and won't drive off with empty tyres, but will have a chance to ponder his choice. Avoid trucks used by artisans and workers, jeeps for people with disabilities, minibuses and ordinary cars, we advised any imitators: aim straight for the SUVs of the rich. They don't serve any practical purpose – SUVs are not so common on Östermalm because of the rugged terrain in that neighbourhood; rarely do they leave the soft carpet of the city asphalt – but emit excessive CO_2 just to flaunt their owners' wealth. We likened SUV drivers to the upper-class youth of Östermalm, who early in the new millennium had developed an infamous habit of purchasing bottles of ultra-expensive Champagne, uncorking them and spraying out the liquid in the neighbourhood's bars, just to show off how much money they could waste – with the difference that this exhaust did more than wet a floor. It killed people.

A wildfire of sorts it was: copycat groups of Indians, or 'tribes' as they would call themselves, appeared across Sweden in the summer and autumn. One night raid could take out 200 SUVs in the inner city of Stockholm, duly followed by a communiqué; 50 in Gothenburg, or a handful in Växjö, or 70 in the posh Western Harbour district of Malmö. It became a media sensation. Appearing at the start of the first cycle of climate activism, just before Al Gore and the IPCC were awarded the Nobel peace prize, national outlets rushed to cover the phenomenon and the local press to print reports of 'the morning after'. The weekend magazine of *Dagens Nyheter*, Sweden's main daily, embedded a reporter in a 'tribe' that worked its way through 'exceedingly SUV-dense quarters', hid when lit up by headlights and continued in silence, operating as but one contingent in a movement under formation, understandable to many, cheered on and emulated by enough numbers to prompt a backlash.

The Indians became objects of fuming indignation. Our actions didn't even do any lasting damage to property; the mildest of nuisances, it imposed on owners the loss of time and money involved in getting the car towed to the gas station or refilling it in situ. But it was pure mortification to some. In their reclining position, the SUVs had about as much stature and purpose as a bin bag, their purpose capsized in flagrant incapacity. It was too much to bear for a segment of owners. 'If I would have seen you "in action" I would have killed you', ran one of the death threats we published on the blog (this was before the age of social media trolling) – 'I and many others put you on the same level as suicide bombers and paedophiles. Indeed I would have preferred to see some paedophiles released and the cells filled with your kind. Disgusting punks, read up a bit before you run around like some fucking guerrilla.' Internet forums for car owners, soldiers, men's sports overflowed with revenge fantasies. There appeared a blog called Cowboys of the Concrete Jungle with pledges to deflate the lungs of Indians. This counterforce disseminated stickers with the image of a boy holding a gun, above which read the words, 'The air in my tyres is private property – deflation is an assault on democracy.' The magazine *Motor Life Today* published a piece on the supposedly ongoing distribution of firearms and live ammunition to SUV owners, warning that many were hunters and military men and expected 'some Indian to bathe in blood any night now'. The vehicles were said to be guarded by 'grim men in dark clothes'. Always the grim men: never far below the surface, the terror of symbolic castration for owners who had invested not only class but manhood in their monster cars.

No violence broke out. Only once did a manly every-day hero chase down an Indian in an underground train, stopping it (rather symbolically) and holding it until police came to arrest the woman. In late September, 'tribes' in Stockholm and Gothenburg responded to the threats with another wave of deflation, dedicated to the half million victims of torrential rains and flooding in Uganda – in solidarity, 'strike at some of the most morbid emissions sources in the Western world', we incited. In the first half of 2007, sales of Volvo SUVs in Sweden had continued their steady rise, but in the second half they plunged by 27 per cent, with similar drops for other models. We took some of the credit for this. When we drew up a balance sheet of the campaign in December, we counted more than 1,500 SUVs temporarily 'disarmed', as we would say. A couple of reports had reached us of owners starting their cars in spite of our precautions; winter was coming, meaning slippery roads, all the more so for the snow being mixed with rain. We didn't want to put lives at risk. Announcing a 'ceasefire', asking SUV owners to reconsider their options in peace, we called off the campaign and pledged to restart it at some later point. Then the cycle turned downwards and towards COP15 in Copenhagen. It came to its sharp end; the Indians of the Concrete Jungle never resumed their activities. I consider that unfortunate.

The deflation of SUVs we luxuriated in was direct action as prank, perhaps too jolly and tender to deserve the term 'sabotage'. All the fossil fuels burnt in the decade since then should bolster the case for more hands-on approaches, and if there is anything to be learned from this little episode, it is that *some exercise of the imagination might allow activists to neutralise CO_2-emitting devices with easily accessed means*. But an objection can be heard: why go after private consumption? Hasn't the movement worked hard to shift attention away from consumers – the favoured subjects of liberal discourse – to the *production* of fossil fuels? Wouldn't pointing to the former represent a slide backwards?

But consumption *is* part of the problem, and most particularly the consumption of the rich. There is a very tight correlation between income and wealth on the one hand and CO_2 emissions on the other. It has been demonstrated from Canada to China: a diminutive share of the population accounts for a wildly outsized portion of the gas released. To be rich in the world today is to come out on top in the distribution of the 'unequal ability to pollute', as Dario Kenner names it in his *Carbon Inequality*. To be super-rich is to own multiple mansions, SUVs and luxury cars, yachts, jets and helicopters and why not also a private airport, a private submarine, a private semi-submersible platform serving as a floating habitat with every desired amenity. After a meticulous study on the level of households, Kenner concludes that '*all rich individuals* in the US and the UK have a significant carbon footprint associated with their lifestyle'. He gives the example of Lord and Lady Bamford, who have a taste for flying guests to parties. In March 2016, they chartered two Boeing jets to take 180 friends on four days of sumptuous celebrations of their birthdays in the palaces of Rajasthan.

On an aggregate level, such lifestyles register as phenomenally skewed emissions, although data constraints – the rich are not always upfront about their emanations – and differences in methodology yield variations. One

Oxfam report from 2015 suggests that the richest 1 per cent of humanity has a carbon footprint 175 times larger than that of the poorest 10 per cent; distending the hierarchy, the richest Americans beat the poorest Mozambicans two thousand times over. One article published by Ilana M. Otto and her colleagues in *Nature Climate Change* in 2019 finds that the richest 0.54 per cent of the species emit one-third more than the poorest half. Another study from the same year hones in on superyachts, defined as yachts longer than 24 metres, often ranging above 70. An estimated 0.0027 per cent of humanity has sufficient assets to purchase even the smallest models. Discounting other environmental damages – such as the superyacht owned by Microsoft cofounder Paul Allen crashing into and trashing 80 per cent of a protected coral reef in January 2016 – this study calculates only the CO_2 emissions from the gasoline burnt to move the superyachts around. The global fleet has 300 vehicles. In a year, it generates as much CO_2 as the 10 million inhabitants of Burundi.

If you want to emit as much CO_2 as possible, there is no faster way than to go on a flying binge. That also comes close to the definition of being rich today. One single flight from London to Edinburgh emits more CO_2 than the average Somalian does in a year; from London to New York, more than the Nigerian and the Nepalese; from London to Perth, more than the Peruvian and the Egyptian, the Kenyan and the Indian. There are fifty-six countries in the world with annual per capita emissions lower than the emissions from one individual flying once between London and New York. These figures work on conservative estimates of the impact of aviation. Who spews this fire from the skies? Even in such a flying-prone country as England, 1 per cent of residents took a fifth of all overseas flights in 2018; 10 per cent took half and *48 per cent none.* But the super-rich prefer their very own planes, or renting one from Warren Buffett, whose fleet of luxury dragons cruise the skies to predictable effect. The private jets operating in the US alone generate as much CO_2 as half of Burundi does in a year.

This family of emissions has a well-attested ethical status. It was first pinpointed in 1991 in a classic essay by two Indian climate scholars and activists, Anil Agarwal and Sunita Narain, who took issue with calculations that treated all emissions as equal. 'Can we really equate', they asked, 'the carbon dioxide contributions of gas guzzling automobiles in Europe and North America or, for that matter, anywhere in the Third World with the methane emissions of draught cattle and rice fields of subsistence farmers in West Bengal or Thailand? Do these people not have a right to live?' A quantum of methane from a ruminant or paddy might have the same radiative forcing as a quantum of CO_2 from an SUV, Agarwal and Narain accepted, but the moral substances are like chalk and cheese.

This insight was then picked up and formalised by Henry Shue, one of the most perceptive philosophers of the climate crisis, who developed a distinction, widely accepted in the literature, between *luxury* and *subsistence* emissions. The former happen because rich people like to wallow in the pleasure of their rank, the latter because poor people try to survive. If a peasant family in India uses coal to cook their food, or light up their house with electricity from a coal-fired power plant, the only available alternative might be no stove and no lamp. Because they are locked in a fossil economy, they have little choice but to use the CO_2-emitting energy on offer. Someone who drives a superyacht cannot be thus exonerated: he could easily abstain from his boat without foregoing a vital need or right, indeed without experiencing any discomfort whatsoever. Subsistence emissions occur in the pursuit of physical reproduction, in the absence of feasible alternatives. Luxury emissions can claim neither excuse. 'People don't need yachts – they want yachts', in the words of a CEO of a top superyacht manufacturer.

Now the border between needs and wants is famously porous, but to ignore the distinction in this context 'is to discard the most fundamental differences in kind that we understand', Shue argued back in 1993. He was grappling with the question of what emissions to cut first. 'We ought', he contended, 'to start with the purely wasteful, frivolous, and superfluous emissions of the affluent engaging in activities they do not need to engage in.' Or, 'even in an emergency one pawns the jewellery before selling the blankets'. This argument was conceived at a critical moment in climate history: in the early 1990s, as the COP summits began to roll, governments were expected to reach a settlement capping global emissions. The thorny issue would be how to divide the allowable remainder between rich and poor. Shue was one of many who argued that the latter could not be required to slam the brake on their development and give up the quest for modern living standards so that the former could continue to fly high; basic decency and the whole scholarly apparatus of justice theory instead demanded that the poor be given *more room to emit*. It was to this end Shue made his distinction. Two decades later, with the COP summits still passively rolling toward disaster, however, he was forced to admit that the situation no longer held.

If, back in the 1990s or early 2000s, the rich governments would have agreed to a ceiling on the aggregate and a shrinking of their quotas – as pretty much everyone else demanded – the poor might indeed have been given some room. But no cap was ever instituted. Global emissions continued to grow by leaps and bounds. The rise in temperature on Earth is a function of cumulative emissions since the time of the steam-engine; the more emitted, the hotter it gets, which is why one can draw up something like a carbon budget. COP25 and counting, the thirtieth anniversary of epochal uselessness approaching, all reasonable carbon budgets are close to depletion. There is not much room left for anyone. 'No one, rich or poor', can have something like a right to emit because all emissions must be brought to zero in no time. Luckily, this does not condemn the poor to eternal poverty, for what they need is not emissions but energy, and with the renewable kind cheaper across the board, the transition does not require the sacrifice of their material aspirations. But where does this leave the distinction between luxury and subsistence emissions? Has it now lost its relevance?

To the contrary. Luxury emissions become more atrocious at the tail-end of carbon budgets, for at least six reasons. First, the harm they inflict is now immediate. Enjoying a day out on a steam yacht in 1913 was not yet a great offence as such, because relatively little CO_2 had been accumulated in the atmosphere, the concentration still hanging below 300 ppm; the addition from the chimney did not supercharge a hurricane or set the match to a dry forest. But when the atmosphere is already glutted with CO_2, extravagant excesses have those directly injurious effects, which means, to skip the euphemisms, that they send projectiles flying towards randomly chosen poor people. The rich could claim ignorance in 1913. Not so now. A group of American and British criminologists have consequently argued that conspicuous consumption of fossil fuels ought to be classified as a crime. It is aggravated by the circumstance, secondly, that the main source of luxury emissions – the hypermobility of the rich, their inordinate flying and yachting and driving – is what frees them from having to bother with the consequences, as they can always shift to safer locations. To be super-rich and hypermobile above 400 ppm is to dump lethal hazards on others *and* get away from them in one master stroke.

Third, luxury emissions represent the ideological spear of business-as-usual, not only maintaining but *actively championing* the most unsustainable kinds of consumption. This is crime sold as ideal living. Consumption in middling strata is patterned on it, the *nouveau riche* across the world scrambling to join the 0.0027 per cent. The damage done to the planet above 1°C owes something to those who continue to advertise profligate dissipation of its resources as the meaning of life. Fourth, the burning of money has an additional ethical connotation when that money could be diverted to helping the victims of that same burning. Ilona Otto and her colleagues point out that in 2017 alone – according to official rolls – forty-four individuals inherited more than $1 billion each, a total sum of $189 billion. The four largest global funds for financing adaptation to climate impacts approved projects amounting to $2.78 billion. Forty-four individuals thus cashed out sixty-eight times more unearned wealth than what the world's victims of climate catastrophe were allocated, and most likely, some of it went straight to super-yachts and the like – as if the act of injecting poison into the groundwater also coincided with snatching purification tablets out of the hands of slum-dwellers. This compounding of the crime can only intensify at higher levels.

And, fifth, the original insight holds more than ever. If we are ever going to start cutting emissions, on any plausible principles, luxury will have to be the first thing to go. The more gigatons of carbon out there, the fiercer the clashes might be over whose emissions to initially terminate when the hammer finally falls. There is as little room left as there is time to postpone that reckoning. From this condition derives the sixth and last reason: the very special strategic status of luxury emissions. They are supremely demoralising for mitigation efforts. Merely catching sight of a superyacht gliding through the estuary, or hearing about the latest record in private tower construction, or reading about the still-soaring sales figures for the most gas-guzzling cars on the market is enough to break anyone's hope that we will ever bend the curve. *If we cannot even get rid of the most preposterously unnecessary emissions, how are we going to begin moving towards zero?* The more gases accumulated, the more accentuated this centrality. Subsistence emissions must be overcome just as much as any other, but they have none of these features of luxury in a CO_2-saturated world: wanton criminality, insulation from the fallout, waste promotion, withholding of resources for adaptation, persisting in the most odious variants and ostentatiously negating the very notion of cuts. A peasant who emits CH_4 from her paddy or CO_2 from her stove cannot be held morally responsible to anything like a similar degree. Indeed, the more entrenched the fossil economy, the slimmer might be her margin of choice.

It follows that states should attack luxury emissions with axes – not because they necessarily make up the bulk of the total, but because of the position they hold. Otto and her colleagues propose 'compulsory restrictions on household and individual emissions' to humble the rich. Now the likelihood of the ruling classes implementing compulsory restrictions on the consumption of the rich – on themselves, that is – is about the same as them donning leather jackets and proclaiming war communism. Nor is this crime likely to be investigated and prosecuted, for capitalism, as the criminologists note, is all about rewarding and adoring it. Under the current balance of class forces, the average capitalist state with some pretension to care about the climate will rather be inclined to begin at the opposite end: with an attack on subsistence emissions.

This is what Emmanuel Macron, king of climate diplomacy and private luxury, did in France in 2018. The fuel tax that triggered the Gilets Jaunes targeted the cars of the popular classes. Rising rents and house prices had long pushed French workers out of cities, into hinterlands where public transport is chronically underdeveloped and 'so owning a car is essential' to commute to work and access public services. Shue would recognise the situation. Macron's carbon tax weighed five times more heavily on the bottom 10 per cent of the population than on the top – effectively a regressive tax on subsistence, while luxury was released from all restraints by *le Président des riches*. It backfired, as it should. But if other bourgeois governments were to work up Macron's passion for the climate, they can be expected to start fumbling in the same direction. Luxury emissions, long acknowledged as the low-hanging fruits of mitigation, are left dangling, heavy and rotten, without any state daring to touch them. Time to pick up some sticks and knock the fruit down.

It might take attacks on luxury-emitting devices to break the spell cast in the sphere of consumption. Much like divestment has striven to remove the licence from fossil fuel dividends and replace it with a stigma, the purpose here would be to hammer home another ethics: rich people cannot have the right to combust others to death. They might conceive of the air that keeps them bloated as their private property, and on the same principle they should be allowed to strut around with nuclear warheads. Disarmament, indeed, but above all an attempt to break out into the only viable route for mitigation: if we have to cut emissions now, that means *we have to start with the rich*. It lies at the outer edge of the thinkable. And so we might take a leaf from the Fedaiyan, who began their struggle against the Shah at a moment when the workers seemed to stand under 'the absolute domination of the enemy' and felt an 'absolute inability to change the established order', in the words of Amir Parviz Pouyan. In his essay 'On the Necessity of Armed Struggle and the Refutation of the Theory of "Survival" ', he captured the suffocating atmosphere of a regime that seemed unalterable, deterministic, beyond popular influence. Could hope survive under such conditions? 'We must take the offensive in order to survive,' Poyan charged:

> Acts of petty sabotage in locations, establishments or whatever else belongs to the bourgeois, bureaucratic and comprador enemy, in general the rich, would expand the spectrum of initiatives. These acts of

sabotage, as they continue, will especially endanger the very things the enemy is extremely afraid of losing. (. . .) The spell breaks and the enemy looks like a defeated magician.

No other text so jolted the generation of militants that spearheaded the fall of the Shah.

It would be a convenient mistake, however, to think that consumption is a problem exclusively of the super-richest 0.0027 per cent. Not even luxury emissions are their prerogative. SUVs have conquered car markets, with stunning consequences for the planet: in late 2019, the IEA reported that this was the second-largest driver of the increasing global CO_2 emissions since 2010. The power sector came first, the swelling SUV fleet second, beating heavy industry – cement, iron, aluminium – and aviation and shipping by wide margins. If SUV drivers were a nation, in 2018 they would have ranked seventh for CO_2 emissions. The incessantly growing share of SUV sales offset all gains from fuel efficiency and electric vehicles; so large and so heavy, these cars continued to devour prodigious amounts of gasoline, as well as energy in the stage of manufacturing. But the latter was excluded from the IEA's calculations. Had they been included, the climatic destructivity would have been even more pronounced in the data, and this for a commodity that serves no discernible human need: safety inside these tanks is an illusion, as SUV drivers are far more likely than other motorists to crash, roll in a crash and die. As the IEA noted, these monsters have sold so well around the world because 'they are considered symbols of wealth and status'. A planet incinerated by the rich, and by the desire to count among them.

Sales have skyrocketed in the global North in nicely symmetrical parallel with the climate crisis. SUVs first seized the US, reaching 63 per cent of car sales in 2016 (the seventh consecutive year of total sales gains – 'an unprecedented string', according to analysts). In Europe, the 'Chelsea tractors' made their entry in the early 2000s, just before the first cycle of climate activism; at its end, in 2009, they had taken 7 per cent of the market. That share stood at 36 per cent in 2018 and was projected to reach 40 per cent three years later. Growth was no less marked in Sweden, where SUV sales jumped 20 per cent in the five short years between 2013 and 2018. No Indians then attempted to halt the trend.

Auto producers constantly roll out new models and spend lavish amounts advertising them. But the movement is on their track. In September 2019, activists from Ende Gelände and other German outfits mobilised 20,000 people in demonstrations and direct actions against the Internationale Automobil-Ausstellung, the world's largest motor show, in Frankfurt. Never before had the car industry been subject to such indictment. It came on the heels of a series of lethal SUV incidents, most dramatically the killing of four people – including a sixty-four-year-old woman and her three-year-old-grandson – by a man who lost control of his luxurious Porsche Macan and slammed into pedestrians on a sidewalk in Berlin. Calls went up for the 'tank-like' cars to be banned. After Angela Merkel had inaugurated the show in Frankfurt, activists climbed on top of SUVs and unfurled banners reading *Klimakiller*. Two months later, the journal *Libération* reported that one street in the sixteenth arrondissement of Paris, home of French high society, had had its SUVs deflated one night. Expect more of that target selection.

It is not entirely correct to say that the movement has refrained from damaging and destroying property. On the night when Donald Trump was elected president, two members of the Des Moines Catholic Worker movement, Jessica Reznicek and Ruby Montoya, trespassed onto a site for construction of the Dakota Access Pipeline in Iowa. They brought coffee canisters filled with rags and motor oil, placed them on the seats of six pieces of heavy machinery and lit matches; five of the six were burnt out in the attack. Autodidacts in the field, Reznicek and Montoya then learnt to use welding-torches with oxygen and acetylene to burn through the steel in the pipes. Protective gear on, they raided the pipeline up and down the state in the spring of 2017 and pierced holes in it, compressing each hit-and-run strike into the span of seven minutes. Then they returned to arson. Equipment at multiple sites were set on fire with parcels soaked in gasoline. The property they attacked belonged to Energy Transfer, a conglomerate of pipeline companies on whose boards one could find Rick Perry, secretary of energy under Trump.

Reznicek and Montoya had immersed themselves in the movement against the Dakota Access Pipeline centred on Standing Rock; they reacted to defeat not by capitulating, but by moving on to the next phase. As the two Catholic workers explained in their communique,

> After exploring and exhausting all avenues of process, including attending public commentary hearings, gathering signatures for valid requests for Environmental Impact Statements, participating in civil disobedience, hunger strikes, marches and rallies, boycotts and encampments, we saw the clear deficiencies of our government to hear the people's demands.

Eventually they resolved to come out and confess. 'We are speaking publicly to empower others to act boldly, with purity of heart, to dismantle the infrastructure which deny us our rights to water, land and liberty,' Reznicek and Montoya announced at a press conference. Their sabotage delayed construction of the pipeline for an uncertain number of months, but no matter how frequently they perforated it, two individuals, of course, could not on their own bring down the juggernaut. That would have required organised upscaling.

In Germany, the conflict over the Hambach forest came to a head in September 2018, when police moved in to clear the way for the brown coal mine. A village in the canopy first had to be torn down. Over several years, activists had built some 60 treehouses, up to 25 metres high, forming interlinked communities or 'barrios' in permanent protection of the forest. The police needed cranes to reach them. The first company to be contracted withdrew after dissent among the staff, the second after public pressure. The third rent out its cranes to cops so they could swing up in the air to catch the activists and crash their tripods, cabins and two-storey villas in scenes eliciting outrage over the things the state would do for coal. Then someone entered the warehouse of this third company and set it on fire. The action was repeated at another depot. Meanwhile, the German branch of Friends of the Earth frantically pushed a lawsuit against the coal company in the regional court, which, in a surprise victory for the movement, ordered a stop to the clearance pending a verdict. Fifty thousand people gathered on a field next to the forest to celebrate the reprieve and reassert the commitment to defeat coal; as of this writing, the tree-houses are rebuilt, the barrios inhabited, the groves still alive with insects and birds.

The Hambach tree squatters have been waging low-intensity conflicts with police and companies, sometimes conducting petty sabotage in and around the groves. The Zone à défendre (ZAD) in France used militant tactics in its successful struggle against the planned airport north of Nantes. Another few cases notwithstanding, the movement has by and large left property destruction an untried tactic. What if it became more than a one-off occurrence? What if hundreds or thousands followed in the footsteps of Reznicek and Montoya? On what grounds could that be cause for regret and condemnation? One might argue that it would open the dams of violence, or even ad lib terrorism. As for the former, Reznicek and Montoya hotly dispute that their actions fell into that category: 'The oil being taken out of the ground and the machinery that does it and the infrastructure which supports it – this is violent', Reznicek stated in an interview. 'We never at all threatened human life. We're acting in an effort to save human life, to save our planet, to save our resources. And nothing was ever done by Ruby or me outside of peaceful, deliberate and steady loving hands.' In the Catholic Worker tradition, ennobled by the Berrigan brothers who used blood and napalm to destroy draft files during the Vietnam War and spoiled nuclear warheads during the late Cold War, righteous property destruction falls within the boundaries of non-violence.

The position has scriptural support. Jesus Christ was no stranger to the tactic: the Gospel of John tells us that he became so infuriated at the sight of money-changers raking in profit from selling cattle in the temple that he used 'a whip of cords' to drive them all out, before pouring out their coins and overturning their tables. Some support can also be found in secular philosophy. It has been argued that the similarity between breaking the bone of a child and breaking the bone of a table is deceptive: only the child can feel pain. Only she can be traumatised, only her dignity violated; the table is devoid of interests and mental states. Physical force that injures inanimate objects does not, on this view, count as violence, because it cannot have the results that constitute the *prima facie* wrongness of what we call violence. At a minimum, those on the receiving end must be sentient beings.

Far more common, however, is the opposite view. One much-cited philosophical essay says that violence 'is always *done*, and it is always done *to* something, typically a person, animal, or piece of property'. The latter class of objects – windows, automobiles, places of business – might be subjected to breaking, burning, stone-throwing and an array of other violent acts. But what about the ordered demolition of a dilapidated house, or the controlled burning of a garden patch? To meet the criteria, the physical attacks damaging or destroying property have to be 'highly vigorous, or incendiary, or malicious', the latter the weightiest attribute. In a similar vein, Ted Honderich defines political violence as 'a use of physical force that injures, damages, violates or destroys people or things, with a political and social intention'. Chenoweth and Stephan submit that 'violent tactics include bombings, shootings, kidnappings, physical sabotage such as the destruction of infrastructure, and other types of physical harm of people and property', which makes it even more impressive that they can name a single case of non-violence. The fall of the Berlin Wall? People didn't caress the cement.

But strategic pacifists are right in asserting that in the eyes of the public, in the early twenty-first century and particularly in the global North, property destruction does tend to come off as violent. Likewise, most people would think of a whip of chords as a weapon and the chasing away of money-changers and overturning of their tables as a minor whirlwind of violence. One should not succumb to an *argumentum ad populum*, but neither should one ascribe meaning to words that deviate too much from the common language. If we were to exclude objects from the definition of violence, we would have to try to convince the world that a crowd of Gilets Jaunes marching down the Champs-Élysées and pulverising every retail store along the way would in fact be practising non-violence – more than a conceptual stretch, a waste of rhetorical effort.

We must accept that property destruction is violence, insofar as it intentionally exerts physical force to inflict injury on a thing owned by someone who does not want it to happen (such as Rick Perry and his fellow Energy Transfer shareholders). But in the very same breath, we must insist on it being *different in kind* from the violence that hits a human (or an animal) in the face, for the reasons just specified: one cannot treat a car cruelly or make it cry. It has no rights truncated in the moment of incineration. Some harm befalls the person behind the car – the driver, the owner – who is prevented from using it as he wishes. But it would be something else to set fire *to him*. Martin Luther King – his moral compass a wonder of reliability next to Gandhi's – endorsed this distinction in his apologia for the urban riots of 1967: 'Violent they certainly were. But the violence, to a startling degree, was focused against property rather than against people', and within the genus of violent acts, this made all the difference: 'A life is sacred. Property is intended to serve life, and no matter how much we surround it with rights and respect, it has no personal being.' Why were the rioters 'so violent with property then? Because property represents the white power structure, which they were attacking and trying to destroy.'

On the standard view, which also seems to be King's, an inanimate object can undergo violence by virtue of being property – standing in a relation, that is, to a human being, who can claim to be indirectly hurt when it is hurt. Shattering a rusty chassis discarded on a dumpsite would scarcely be violent, since no one would be around to sustain the loss. But this indirectness is also what sets property destruction apart, for one cannot equate the treatment of people with the treatment of the things they own. Even the man most deeply in love with his car should admit that slicing up its tyres and slicing up his lungs come with separate ethical tags. Only the most extreme form of bourgeois fetishism – claiming that the owned object is in fact animate – could muster a case against this differentiation. There is, however, one exception, one type of property destruction that approaches killing and maiming, namely that which hits material conditions for subsistence: poisoning someone's groundwater, burning down a family's last remaining grove of olive trees or, for that matter, firebombing a paddy field in an Indian peasant village because it emits methane would come close to a stab in the heart. At the other end of the spectrum is the blasting of a superyacht into smithereens.

Now if we accept that property destruction is violence, and that it is less grave than violence against humans, this in itself neither condemns nor condones the practice. It seems that it ought to be avoided for as long as possible. Even a revolutionary Marxist should regard it as *prima facie* wrong, because private property is the form in which capitalism snares productive forces that often – although at a falling rate – cater to some human needs. We would not want a situation where people went around throwing bricks into cafés and toppling school walls and slitting jackets on a whim, just for the hell of it. Highly pressing circumstances must rather be present for attacks on property to come under consideration. Then begins the act of balancing.

'Is not a woman's life, is not her health, are not her limbs more valuable than panes of glass?' asked Emmeline Pankhurst. Or, in the words of one philosopher mulling over violent civil disobedience: if a grossly immoral war is being waged, the right of railway engineers to keep the tracks in good shape may be superseded by 'the more important right of the people in the country to which the troops are headed, to life itself'. In the climate breakdown, the scales might tip quickly – on the one side, things like pipelines and diggers and SUVs; on the other, a weight that must tend towards the infinite because *it encompasses all values*. A woman's life, her health and limbs, the right of a people to life itself and everything else is in peril. Because of the temporal dimension, moreover, Pankhurst's question must also be posed from the standpoint of future generations: will those in school today or born next year grow up to think that the machines of the fossil economy were accorded insufficient respect? Or will they look back on this moment in time rather like we, or at least those of us with a modicum of feminist leanings, look back on the suffragettes and see smashed windows as a price worth paying? But when suffragettes broke panes, torched letter-boxes and hammered on paintings, these things had, in and of themselves, at most a tangential relation to the problem of male monopoly on the vote. Now the machines of the fossil economy *are* the problem.

One might turn to contemporary scholarship on civil disobedience and political violence for further guidance. William Smith, one of the most astute theorists, has recently turned his attention to direct action along the lines of 'occupations, sabotage, property damage and other types of force' designed to dissuade opponents from proceeding with their plans and deter them from duplicating their efforts. He regards this taxon of action as distinct from civil disobedience, with its emphasis on moral suasion. When could it ever be justified? He sets up three criteria. First,

> direct action should be limited to disrupting prac-
> tices that might result in, or imminently threaten to
> generate, serious and irreversible harm. The urgency
> of the situation might be sufficient to override a
> presumption in favour of lawful advocacy or civil
> disobedience, if too much damage would occur

before the process of reflection and reconsideration
triggered by the latter could run its course.

It should be noted that this argument is not tailored for
the climate crisis, which receives no mention.

Second, there must be grounds for believing that
mellower tactics have led nowhere, and that this lack of
progress is itself a symptom of the structural depth of
the ills. Third, there should be, at least ideally, some
higher charter, convention or edict the wrongdoers have
flouted and violated and that the activists can refer to.
Thanks to three decades of institutionalised logorrhoea,
there are no scarcities here: from the UNFCCC to the
Paris Agreement, not to speak of the ceremoniously
promulgated national pledges and plans (at least in
Europe), whole libraries' worth of covenants and
consensuses have been assembled for climate activists to
pursue the felons with. But Smith concedes that all
three criteria need not be fully satisfied. 'The severity or
urgency of the harm' may be such that direct action
needs no further warrant.

There is nothing madly aberrant about this radicalism;
rather, the literature is replete with similar deductions.
Nor is Smith alone in claiming that the right to resistance
at some point can morph into a duty. In fact, once the
gravity of the climate crisis is duly recognised, it is difficult
to see what ethical precepts could be marshalled to keep
that morphing at bay and uphold a ban on destroying the
causative property. To date, no case has been made for the

precedence of the physical integrity of CO_2-emitting devices.

What of terrorism? We have seen Lanchester speculate about a scenario where people scratch SUVs with their keys and subsume it under that term. Is that appropriate? Few other concepts are as loaded with ideology or coloured by a particular moment; 'violence' has a history as old as the mists of time, but 'terrorism' can now hardly be uttered without the likes of Donalds Rumsfeld and Trump ventriloquising. Less reason, then, to make concessions to ordinary usage. If terrorism is to have any analytical substance, its core definition must be *the deliberately indiscriminate killing of innocent civilians for the purpose of instilling terror* or something very nearly like it. We have rejected the claim of Jessica Reznicek and Ruby Montoya to be non-violent – should we also label them terrorists? On this definition, it would be risible.

In just war theory, the *differentia specifica* of terrorism, the particular moral transgression that blackens its name, is the failure to discriminate between combatants and non-combatants when killing people. Reznicek and Montoya didn't kill combatants. They killed no one, injured nobody, touched not a hair on anyone's head, and so they must be placed at the farthest remove from the category of terrorism. Someone who would brand them terrorists would in all likelihood refuse to extend the term to people who invest or indulge in CO_2-emitting devices, thus recommending that acts that wound no living beings be deemed terrorism and acts that actually, certifiably kill people be absolved. Such conceptual abuse from the guardians of business-as-usual would not be in the slightest surprising. Indeed it seems to have already begun, in anticipation of the onset of property destruction at scale: in 2019, the Danish and Swedish intelligence services and their academic mouthpieces warned that 'climate terrorism is on the horizon', in the words of Magnus Ranstorp, ideological hitman of the repressive state apparatus in Sweden, who had never before spilled a public word on the climate question and did not, of course, refer to the combustion of fossil fuels. He and his fellows had acts like Reznicek's and Montoya's on their radar. 'One can easily imagine', one Danish expert opined on the activists of the third cycle, 'that they become frustrated with a political system that does not in their eyes take this matter seriously enough, and a small portion of them might resort to violent actions', this hypothetical scenario being sketched in May 2019. Behold the paradox.

This is obviously not to suggest that CO_2 emissions should be categorised as acts of terrorism, which would also constitute conceptual abuse, although arguably of a lesser sort, insofar as blind killing is central to what terrorism is. The term should not be devaluated, the crime not trivialised. Someone who enters a mosque with the intention to kill the maximum number of worshippers is undertaking an act of terrorism; someone who drills a hole in a pipeline or sets a depot aflame performs 'a categorically distinct act', in the words of Steve Vanderheiden, leading philosopher of environmental ethics. One could retort that the latter also seeks to create an atmosphere of fear. Is not the idea here to *terrorise* capitalists into submission? But the establishment of a deterrence cannot be a sufficient condition for terrorism. It is common knowledge that the prison system exists to deter citizens from infractions of the law, by threatening to abolish their freedom of movement; closed-circuit TV cameras, armed guards and a panoply of other fully normalised phenomena have similar functions. Parents have told lurid tales, raised their voice, even smacked their children to inculcate fear for unwholesome things. All of this might be objected to; none of it can be called terrorism. The unique objective of the mosque killer is to create an atmosphere where Muslims *fear for their lives* and go to Friday prayer in the knowledge that they could be killed at any moment just because of who they are. Fear for the loss of property is a categorically distinct fear. It pertains to the balance sheet and budget, not the body.

'Vandalism' would be a more appropriate term, as would 'sabotage', which we have used as a synonym for the damage and destruction of property; as long as no blood is shed, this is the palette to choose from. It changes the moment blood is shed. This could happen, by mistake or design. It does not have to. In 2004, two scholars working for the Norwegian defence establishment searched through 5,000 recorded incidents of terrorism and found 262 cases of what they called 'petroleum terrorism', defined as attacks on oil infrastructure and personnel, concentrated in the Middle East, Nigeria and Colombia (of those attacks, one (1) had been conducted by environmentalists). Only 11 per cent resulted in any casualties, usually one or two. Removing the attacks on personnel, the casualty figures all but disappeared. The deadly attacks had primarily been conducted by Islamists – as in the Algerian civil war – who felt few compunctions about bloodletting, whereas leftist and other secular groups, including the European anti-imperialist front of the 1980s, tended to eschew it. The occurrence of deaths and injuries in conjunction with 'petroleum terrorism' could thus, the Norwegians concluded, 'be explained by differences in ideology'. But that doesn't mean that Islamists have to kill when they attack oil: the drones diving into Abqaiq did not produce a single recorded injury to a human body.

The fine art to be mastered here is that of controlled political violence. When the townships boiled after the Sharpeville massacre, Nelson Mandela tried to convince his fellow ANC leaders that 'violence would begin whether we initiated it or not. Would it not be better to guide this violence ourselves, according to principles where we saved lives by attacking symbols of oppression, and not people?' Sages like Ranstorp may have spotted a similar ferment (though the similarities clearly shouldn't be exaggerated). When Mandela weighed the options, they included terrorism and guerrilla warfare, but 'terrorism inevitably reflected poorly on those who used it. Guerrilla warfare was a possibility, but since the ANC had been reluctant to embrace violence at all, it made sense to begin with the form of violence that inflicted the least harm against individuals: sabotage.'

At the moment of this writing, when the third cycle is steadily coursing upwards, in a political climate still haunted by al-Qaeda and Daesh, it would be catastrophic for the movement if any part of it used terrorism. The same could go for unintended casualties and injuries. The moral capital the climate movement has amassed could be depreciated or obliterated in one blow. If killing has bad consequences for the right cause, its *prima facie* impermissibility is not attenuated but amplified, and so any climate militant who contemplates sabotage should abide by the original rules of the MK 'not to endanger life in any way' – or, with William Smith, they should be 'constrained, proportionate and discriminating'. She should warn people of the risk of the injury where applicable, desist from harassing or intimidating persons, take precautions to avoid damage to the environment. Can such restraints be guaranteed? Obviously not. Like all tactical choices, they must be forged in the moment. Jessica Reznicek and Ruby Montoya are tutors in this department, dismantling fossil fuel infrastructure with 'steady loving hands.'

I once asked Bill McKibben, after an energising speech to a capacity crowd, when – given that the situation is as urgent as he portrayed it and we all know it is – we escalate. He was visibly ill at ease. The first part of his response presented what we might call the objection from asymmetry: as soon as a social movement engages in violent acts, it moves onto the terrain favoured by the enemy, who is overwhelmingly superior in military capabilities. The state loves a fight of arms; it knows it will win. Our strength is in numbers. This is a pet argument for strategic pacifists, but it is disingenuous. Violence is not the sole field where asymmetry prevails. The enemy has overwhelmingly superior capabilities in virtually *all* fields, including media propaganda, institutional coordination, logistical resources, political legitimacy and, above all, money. If the movement should shun uphill battles, a divestment campaign seems like the worst possible choice: trying to sap fossil capital by means of capital.

There is a centuries- or even millennia-long history of slingshots downing Goliaths and other tactics ingenious enough to find cracks in the enemy's armour. As part of the mass resistance in the besieged Gaza Strip in the spring of 2018, Palestinians invented techniques for sending kites and helium-inflated condoms carrying incendiary materials across the wall to burn Israeli property. The most powerful state in the Middle East, armed to the teeth with atomic bombs and the most sophisticated systems for intercepting rockets, stood helpless before these lumpen missiles from the most thoroughly deprived fragment of a people. In the popular uprisings that swirled across the globe in 2019, not only did crowds smash boutiques in Beirut with iron bars, set fire to SUVs in the posh neighbourhoods overlooking Port-au-Prince, throw themselves into ferocious clashes with police in Quito – the largest pipeline in Ecuador shut down after indigenous protesters 'disrupted' it – burn banks and official buildings in Iran and Iraq and rip up the civil resistance model day after day. They also revelled in creative new-old technologies of warfare without guns. In Santiago, they used up to fifty handheld lasers to bring down police drones from the sky. In Hong Kong, they filled streets with 'mini Stonehenges' – one brick laid horizontally over two standing ones – to block the paths of police vehicles, and built giant wooden catapults, medieval-style, to fling petrol bombs towards the lines of the Chinese state. No law says that asymmetry in *this* field can never be overturned from below, nor that violence must conflict with the strength of numbers. Rather, unarmed collective violence is one expression of that strength, one way of bringing down the seemingly invincible. Property destruction has always been essential to it. Can it ever acquire mass proportions in the climate struggle? Only if the movement first overcomes the taboo against it.

Then there is the objection from time, quick to make an appearance: we have not yet exhausted non-violence. We have to be patient. We must give perfectly civil disobedience another chance and let it mature for more years if needed; it must not be ditched ahead of time. But in this case, a charge of rashness could scarcely stick. Due to the temporality of the problem, again, the opposite objection – a surfeit of patience until now – would fit better. 'We live in a dream world', George Monbiot once observed:

Our dreaming will, as it has begun to do already, destroy the conditions necessary for human life on Earth. Were we governed by reason, we would be on the barricades today, dragging the drivers of Range Rovers and Nissan Patrols out of their seats, occupying and shutting down the coal-burning power stations, bursting in upon the Blairs' retreat from reality in Barbados and demanding a reversal of economic life as dramatic as the one we bore when we went to war with Hitler.

Those words were written in 2003.

But not everyone can mix a Molotov cocktail or fill a coffee canister with motor oil! This is the objection from demography, averring that non-violence is inherently attractive to the masses and violence exclusionary. At first sight, it also seems disingenuous, for we do not normally think that activities requiring special skills and physical competences should, for that very reason, be renounced; no one saved by a firefighter would complain that he should have stayed at home, because not everyone has his fitness and agility. Social processes tend to involve divisions of labour. At a closer look, however, the objection carries more force, for it deals not with technical but with *political* relations and arrangements, and here mass participation is a value in itself, unlike in an operating theatre. And empirically speaking, overall, Chenoweth and Stephan are correct in claiming that 'barriers to participation are much lower for non-violent resistance than for violent insurgency'. The festive atmosphere in a square taken over by protesters has more to speak for it and less to scare people away than a mayhem of stone-throwing. This is one reason why 1.) non-violent mass mobilisation should (where possible) be the first resort, militant action the last; and 2.) no movement should ever voluntarily suspend the former, only give it appendages.

That said, the mass appeal of the civil disobedience etiquette can be overblown. XR has gone out of its way to shower the police in love. 'Police, we love you – it's for your children too', ran a common chant in London. After the action in Malmö in September 2019, the local branch of the Rebellion posted a picture of an activist and a cop having a tête-à-tête, all smile and affection, and confirmed that 'at the end of the day, we're all in the same boat'. In the handbook, we learn that Rebels should seek to 'actively try to get arrested' and that this desire is 'at the heart of Extinction Rebellion'. Well this appeals to *some* people. As pointed out in an open letter to XR after the London 'spring uprising' in 2019, written by the Wretched of the Earth, a network of climate activists of colour, together with Ende Gelände, the Hambach forest occupation and a plethora of other allies, throwing oneself into the arms of the police is a sign of privilege. People from racialised communities might hesitate to do so. Middle-class whites can count on the good manners of the cops; working-class Muslims and blacks and migrants without papers don't have that assurance. This might be one reason why XR, in its first year of existence, was plagued by a whiteness out of all proportion to the demographics in cities like London and Malmö. Others would feel summoned by a more confrontational or evasive approach to the repressive state apparatus. At the end of the day, as the Wretched of the Earth asserted, we are too many and too manifold to fit into one boat: the only vessel that can make room for the level of participation required to win this 'fight of our lives' is '*a diversity and plurality of tactics*'. Yes, such diversity and plurality will open for internal tensions, which no movement that has altered the course of history has done without. There is something suspicious about total tactical conformity.

Taken from the reading of movements against dictatorships, a related objection cites democracy: violence is detrimental to the goal of peaceful, constitutional deliberation. If the enemy is beaten up or worse, he is expelled from the circle of the rightful inheritors of the nation and won't come back to sit at the table as he should. (Chenoweth and Stephan add that foreign investors will be frightened.) But in the kind of struggle the climate movement is waging – against a set of productive forces flourishing in mature democracies – this argument loses some of its applicability. It loses the rest when we consider only the type of violence reserved for property, as another philosopher has elucidated: 'seizing and destroying the gold-encrusted jet of a plutocrat is an eminently striking and symbolic form of protest', and 'given that the plutocrat himself is not threatened', no anti-democratic ostracism takes place.

The second part of McKibben's response advanced the objection from popular support. As soon as violence is thrown into the mix, it evaporates. The movement can win sympathy by clasping hands around the White House, or blocking a gas terminal with a fleet of canoes, or staging a die-in in a natural history museum, but it can only repel the public by burning things or clashing with cops. There is clearly a grain of truth to this, particularly in the US. France is different. A French social movement does not automatically become a pariah if it spices up mass mobilisation with some property destruction and rioting: there is no biological law of repellence, even in the global North. Rather, we face an ostensible paradox here, in that the US is a vastly more violent society – as measured by the diffusion of guns, the incidence of mass shootings, the civilians killed by police, the veneration of armed heroes in popular culture, the belligerence of the state and any other yardstick – than France, and yet the intolerance for violence committed by social movements is at its highest in the former. But the paradox dissolves when we consider that the US swept the slate clean for unrestrained capitalism by means of genocidal violence. France, on the other hand, still has a perennially renewed legacy of popular upheaval and a comparatively combative working class. The tolerance for subaltern violence stands in inverse relation to the absoluteness of capitalist dominance and the consequent suffusion of a social formation with violence – the American allergy, in other words, is a pathology.

Americans, however, aren't the only ones who live in sick societies, and activists obviously have to learn how to behave inside them without instantly alienating their intended audiences. But neither should they take public aversion to even the softest sabotage as a natural fact. Levels of receptivity are contingent on time, and this must hold in particular for the climate struggle. If in the still-not-so-hot year of 2007, the Indians of the Concrete Jungle could deflate SUV tyres in Sweden without incurring any losses in support for the climate movement – it was the Cowboys that were up in arms – then what forms of sabotage could not go down well, even in this most depoliticised of social formations, in 2025 or 2040? At six degrees, the itch to blow up pipelines might be well-nigh universal among whatever humanity remains. We should posit *a law of a tendency of the receptivity to rise* in a rapidly warming world; anything else would be to presume a species-wide death wish. If fossil fuels continue to be combusted and temperatures to climb, physical attacks on the sources of the more and more dreadful, less and less deniable calamities should resonate with broader and broader layers. The only thing that could interfere with this tendency would be an actual annulment of business-as-usual, a Green New Deal or some similar policy package breaking the curve and moving it towards zero – then property destruction would appear superfluous to very many. This would of course be the best-case scenario, to which all efforts should contribute. In its absence, receptivity must go up, from however low levels, because

should be the moment to strike and stretch: next time the wildfires burn through the forests of Europe, take out a digger. Next time a Caribbean island is battered beyond recognition, burst in upon a banquet of luxury emissions or a Shell board meeting. The weather is already political, but it is political *from one side only*, blowing off the steam built up by the enemy, who is not made to feel the heat or take the blame. It is part of Lanchester's paradox that climate activists have yet to time their actions to singular climate catastrophes. Capacity could be held in reserve.

The same temporality may swiftly move the benchmark of moderation, as it did during the civil rights era: Martin Luther King appeared radical in the late 1950s, Extinction Rebellion in 2019. With the emergence of a flank, positions shift. That is when progress can be made: when representatives of XR sit down with the British government to negotiate a path to zero emissions by 2025 – perhaps the ministers will insist on 2028 – some mitigation would finally be underway. To end up on that table, XR or its equivalents might need a little unrequested assistance, just as MLK once did. It is the duty of the erstwhile radicals to denounce the new flank and accuse it of undermining their endeavours. If they were to applaud the troublemakers who threaten or commit acts of violence, they would not gain the edge of respectability and receive no invitation to the policy-making chambers. A positive radical flank effect presupposes, with Haines, 'a division of labor in which moderates and radicals perform very different roles': the latter stoke up the crisis to a breaking-point, the former offer a way out. It follows that prospective militants should expect and even hope for condemnation from the mainstream, without which the two would become indistinguishable and the effect be lost. Put differently, they should not try to convince XR or Bill McKibben or any other part of the movement committed to absolute non-violence to pick up the cocktails and the canisters – it's not their job. It's the job of the factions to come.

There is, however, as Haines and others have demonstrated and McKibben apprehended, also a palpable risk for a *negative* radical flank effect. Extremism can make a movement look so distasteful as to deny it all influence. There is no lack of examples of movements shooting themselves in the foot. Because of the magnitude of the stakes in the climate crisis, negative effects could be unusually ruinous here. Militant formations on the flank of this movement would thus have to be *especially* circumspect and mindful of the principles laid down by, for instance, William Smith: practitioners of direct action are responsible before their 'community of opinion' and bound by the duty to advance, not retard, its cause. They may dive into a campaign of property destruction on condition of being prepared to amend or call it off, if it becomes clear that it will draw too much retaliation, vilification, embarrassment on the movement. Now this presents militants with a genuine dilemma. On the one hand, they have to trust the mainstream to reproach and disown them – a seal of the division of labour – but on the other, there might be no better source of information about deleterious consequences for the movement as a whole. When do they ignore the censure and proceed, satisfied? When do they hear it and adjust? If not a catch-22, it is certainly another tightrope. But then no one said militancy should be casual or comfortable.

The same applies to the inevitable objection from the standpoint of repression. Why provoke the state to rain down its harshest measures on the movement? In October 2019, Jessica Reznicek and Ruby Montoya were indicted on charges that carried a sentence of 110 years in prison. The previous year, a panel at a conference for oil and gas corporations in Houston, Texas, discussed the looming danger of sabotage and the need for the state to throttle it. Kelcy Warren – CEO of Energy Transfer, fossil fuel billionaire, supporter of Perry and Trump – took direct aim at the two women: 'I think you're talking about some-body who needs to be removed from the gene pool.' For Reznicek and Montoya, the prospect of 110 years in prison appeared to fall in the category – again related to faith – of sacrifice, although not of the kind that passively takes on unearned suffering. They risked the most draco-nian punishment *in the act of resistance* and were ready to pay the price. Should they be upbraided for the choice? Chenoweth and Stephan hold it against violent resistance that it mandates 'high levels of both commitment and risk tolerance', which are not for everyone. But seen from another angle, the consequent sacrifice is a signal to others that *this is worth fighting for*, even spending the rest of one's life in prison for, and the climate crisis could do with some more acts of that calibre. So far, few have been prepared to risk more than a couple of nights under arrest. Compared with what struggling people in history have gone through, the comfort levels of climate activism in the global North must be deemed fairly high, which does not quite bespeak the significance of the problem.

Perhaps more people than Reznicek and Montoya will eventually find the motivation. It does not require a willingness to submit to the law – to the contrary, that familiar paragraph in the civil disobedience protocol is becoming more obsolete by the day, as a ruling order that destroys the foundations of life deserves no loyalty from its subjects. Sabotage can proceed in the dark. Indeed, if one wants to accomplish something, one shouldn't follow the example of Roger Hallam, who announced *beforehand* that he would fly drones into Heathrow airport to protest its expansion, with the predictable result that he was pre-emptively apprehended. The stronger it gets, the more the movement will have to wrestle intimately with these forces of repression, even if it stays with the most non-violent tactics: in August 2018, for example, an activist paddling in the vicinity of a pipeline in Louisiana was handcuffed by private security and thrown into a court system that threatened her with five years in prison. Laws with heavy penalties for *every* protest against pipelines have made their way through more than a dozen US states in the Trump era. During the 'autumn uprising' of 2019, the London police banned all protests under the XR flag. Criminalisation of non-violent climate protests is 'on the horizon', to speak with Ranstorp. If militancy accelerates it to an indefensibly harmful degree, we would have a negative radical flank effect. If it spreads regardless, the movement would face a choice that so many others have encountered before: back down or continue to fight, diversify, combine underground and overground work and do not yield. Love-bombing the police with flowers would not then necessarily be the surest way to advance.

When tens of thousands of activists are engaged in lawbreaking, some errors are to be expected. During its two-weeks-long 'autumn uprising', XR had approximately 30,000 people out on the streets of London to create maximum annoyance and disturbance; perhaps a lapse was unavoidable. Its target and manner of execution were not. In the morning rush hours of 17 October 2019, a group of XR activists entered the London underground and light rail system to stop the traffic. Two of them brought a ladder into the Canning Town Tube station in the eastern part of the city, placed it against a train, climbed onto the roof and unfolded a banner reading 'Business As Usual = DEATH'. Commuters on the platform were first baffled and then furious. They appear to have belonged to the city's largely non-white working class; on the many films circulating afterwards, one voice can be heard shouting, 'I need to get to work, I have to feed my kids.' The crowd surged towards the train, screaming for the men to come down. One commuter – incidentally a black man, in blue jeans and a plain beanie – tried to climb onto the roof, at which point one of the activists – incidentally a white man, in a suit and a tie – aimed a hard kick at his head. White man on top kicking black man below. The former was then dragged down onto the platform and set upon. Causing an uproar in the city, the incident marked an ignominious end to the 'uprising'.

What constituted this as the stupidest action ever undertaken by the climate movement in the global North, however, was the response by XR London, hub of the global Rebellion. It had the opportunity to wash its hands of the men in the tube, but instead the official statement exonerated the kick-to-the-head as an act of 'self-defence', excused the activists by appealing to their high characters – 'they were a grandfather, an ex-Buddhist teacher, a vicar and a former GP among others' – and defended the action as planned 'within Extinction Rebellion's principles and values, centred around non-violence and compassion'. One of the cofounders went on the BBC to bless the action as 'peaceful' and 'non-violent'. Others in XR London – a majority, according to one poll – vehemently opposed it. Given the amount of self-policing and internalisation of tactical principles the movement has proved itself capable of, however, one has to ask how this slipped through. Three factors are immediately apparent.

First, the strategy of XR has been to wreak generalised – but, mind you, non-violent – havoc on the urban fabric, in the belief that this will force politicians to respond adequately to the crisis; this is how change happens, Hallam and the other readers of Chenoweth and Stephan have adjudicated. The fossil economy is here understood as similar to an autocracy, a category mistake that licenses the targeting of pretty much anything for disruption. Hence the fantastic fallacy of stopping an underground train. It's as if the civil rights movement would have blockaded the entrance to a black Baptist church in Alabama, or Egyptian revolutionaries trooping away from Tahrir to attack an oppositional newspaper. This own goal did not aim at subsistence emissions, in the manner of Macron, but rather at subsistence *non*-emissions; as anyone with rudimentary knowledge of the climate problem will know – and as commuters at Canning Town shouted out – public transport is part of the solution. That climate activists got it into their heads to obstruct it beggars belief.

Second, XR has remained persistently aloof from factors of class and race, remaining based in white middling strata with no standpoint other than their own. Its rhetoric and aesthetics have dripped with a kind of piety and smugness those strata are uniquely prone to – or, as one *Guardian* columnist quipped, 'Why do so many XR occupations look like an audience in search of the National Theatre? And why would an XR campaigner think it persuasive to tweet: "We are engineers. We are lawyers. We are doctors. We are everyone"?' Unlike certain other branches of the movement, anti-capitalism and class antagonism are absent from the XR discourse – these are the Rebels for Life out to topple a mendacious cohort of politicians. With better leaders of the state, open-eyed and true to science, life could be safeguarded. To bring them into place, XR trusts in the conclusion from Chenoweth and Stephan that a certain share of the population – 3.5 per cent is the figure making the rounds – has to be corralled onto the streets. This requires muting or switching off any finger-pointing and rich-bashing rhetoric that could alienate supporters. The Rebellion has thus positioned itself as 'beyond politics', neither left nor right, hailing police as much as ordinary citizens, even pandering to the concerns of conservative constituencies: 'If you believe', says one XR agitprop video, 'in people's right to property and if you believe that the state should keep order and safety for people then you also now have to be against the impacts of catastrophic climate change.' The right should be won over, not confronted.

The problem with this, of course, is that 'the right to property' – more precisely, a very particular but very common type of property – is what must be broken. And the order-keeping state stands in the way. Look at it which way you will, from the angle of investment, production or consumption, it is the rich that drive the emergency, and a climate movement that does not want to eat the rich, with all the hunger of those who struggle to put food on the table, will never hit home. A movement that refuses to make the distinctions between classes and colliding interests will end up on the wrong side of the tracks. *That* is a recipe for alienating precisely the people who have the least to gain from continued business-as-usual. A climate movement without social anger will not acquire the required striking capacity, and it should have no difficulties developing the point – and indeed, some Gilets Jaunes have touted the slogan 'More ice sheets, fewer bankers'. Or, 'End of the month, end of the world: same perpetrators, same fight.' Not only do the rich make our lives miserable, they are working to *terminate* the lives of multitudes. Here is another dimension in which XR leaves room for radical flanks of the movement: those who dare to speak the name of the enemy.

Third, the violence that XR eventually engaged in did not target police or private property, but a black man on the way to his job, and this cannot really be seen as accidental. Nor do we have reason to doubt that if an XR activist had kicked a cop in the head, the repudiation would have been unequivocal. Pacifism has perhaps never existed as a real thing. What exists is the ability, or not, to distinguish between forms of violence. The peculiarity of pacifism is that it imbues its adherents with a self-righteousness, borne out of the fetishisation of one sometimes useful type of tactic. If it stays hegemonic, this doctrine will ensure that the climate movement remains, at best, the distant, well-mannered cousin of social revolt in the 2020s. Here is a contrast from late 2019: Chilean students reacting to the rise in public transport fares – championing that mode of transportation, as free and accessible for all – by organising mass trespassing through the turnstiles, attacking ticket machines, supermarkets and company headquarters and touching off a nationwide uprising against soaring inequalities in the homeland of neoliberalism. Meanwhile, the movement against climate catastrophe:

placid and composed. The exigent strategic task is to wed the latter movement to the forces of the former.

The failure of XR to do so, however, does not detract from its very considerable achievements: in the UK in particular, the two civil disobedience campaigns of 2019 massively shifted the point of gravity in domestic politics. They did more to press home the climate emergency than a thousand additional peer-reviewed papers. Towards the end of the year, public concern about the crisis had reached unheard-of levels, and both the House of Commons and the European Parliament had acceded to one XR demand – officially declaring a climate emergency – although, unsurprisingly, without actual measures corresponding to such a situation. But what was perhaps most awesome about XR was the sheer speed of its development, velocity now being the most needed feature of action. Learning the next steps might come fast too.

But if the temptation to fetishise one kind of tactic should be resisted, this also applies, of course, to property destruction and other forms of violence. The tactic with the greatest potential for this movement might be something different. It might be the climate camp. As I have been writing this text, the Swedish government has been deliberating about the application from Swedegas to pump gas into the country, the process in which the blockade of the Gothenburg harbour intervened. The decision came in this morning: against all expectations, the government turned Swedegas down, with direct reference to the recent protests. We won. It's another one of the small wins so invaluable for this movement, although it might still turn out to be short-lived, like the victory over Keystone XL; a far-right government is likely in the near future in this country too. But every respite, every little intermission in business-as-usual is a reminder that a world – not another world, this world – might still be possible.

Climate camps have a way of building on each other, spreading horizontally, stacking up experiences of how to fight fossil capital on the ground. Unlike the Occupy and similar camps that cropped up in 2011 – to which they are of course related – climate camps are planned long in advance, with fixed dates for erection and dismantling; neither spontaneous nor reactive, they feed into a plotted escalation. Ende Gelände has now raised the ante against German fossil capital for half a decade, while forming cadres that go home to other countries and organise their own camps, and so on. We have yet to see diminishing returns from activist investment; Ende Gelände has continued to draw in larger numbers and outmanoeuvre the police. But such success can be hard to replicate else-where. Fewer than the five to ten thousand now readily drummed up in the Rhineland, activists in other parts of Europe have found that a pre-announced camp can give the corporations time to prepare and move out sufficient fuel and equipment to cushion against a blockade. With the trouble limited, the police may blunt the edge of the action by standing to the side and letting it pass. There is chatter in the movement about combining camps with smaller, secret, surprise hits to cause real disruption. Whatever comes out of it, the climate camp is the unrivalled laboratory for learning this fight.

Anyone who has visited one will have had a taste of the process: the slimy porridges served after the gong is struck in the morning, the rotating peeling of onion, the food shipments miraculously materialising on the railway tracks. A climate camp is its own distinctive amalgam of the archaic and the contemporary – the metallic buzz from a drone filming for the three-minute clip later spread on social media, above outhouses in wooden planks emptied through manual labour. Activists spin on stationary bikes to charge their laptops. Singing, chanting, they fill nets with hay to make cushions for pressing through police cordons and protecting against pepper spray. The mix is of recently politicised youth, seasoned hippies, short-haired dykes, tattooed muscular men, students, precarious workers, anti-fascists, mothers with kids in tow, everyone a degree shabbier than in their daily lives, as on a music festival.

Affinity groups are cemented in drawn-out meetings. Delegates are sent to plenaries and return to share information and canvass opinions; more often than not, the process is frustratingly time-consuming. Human microphones announce the next training session. On the fields, columns line up with the flags of their finger – gold, red, silver, pink – and practise breaking through or passing around obstacles. There is a militaristic quality to this form of non-violence: the officer corps positioned right behind the front banners, communicating with the command through headphones, infantry pressing on from behind. Contingency planning for different scenarios, scouts reporting movements of police and situation at target. Names of lawyers and phones of the legal team are scribbled on arms (no one here wants to get arrested) to the sounds of spray cans tinkling as the coveralls are adorned with the logo of the two crossed hammers. Someone struggles to fix a banner with the words 'Put up a FUCKING fight for what you LOVE'. It has the silhouette of a ponytailed girl kicking a smoking chimney.

And then, in the morning, we march off, in the hundreds or thousands, bags packed, torches flaring, the chants keeping a steady beat – 'who shut shit down? we shut shit down!' – and hours later, invariably, we reach the mine, the tracks, the terminal. Sometimes, as we hold our positions around a complex of power plants, we can see the smoke from the chimneys thin out. It dies down. And then it is gone.

3

Fighting Despair

If both protest and resistance seem vain, there is always an alternative ready at hand: to give up on humanity and this planet. It already has its exponents. One of them is Roy Scranton, whose claim to fame is a book called *Learning to Die in the Anthropocene*, followed by *We're Doomed. Now What?* He is adamant that 'we're fucked'. It's too late already – 'too late to stop apocalyptic global warming'; we have 'passed the point where we could have done anything about it'; we are 'already over the cliff' and now stare into the chasm of 'endless, depthless, unassuageable human suffering'. It 'ends in disaster, no matter what'. All that is left is learning to die. The exact identity of the entity that needs to learn to die is somewhat doubtful; Scranton slides between the individual, civilisation, capitalist civilisation and the human species, a conflation of a most symptomatic nature. It is hard for him to ever distinguish between these scales.

What is never in doubt, however, is the futility of protest and resistance: pervading Scranton's writings is a disdain for collective action. He describes the vacuous feeling of marching alongside 400,000 other atomised individuals in the People's Climate March – a waste of time, showcasing 'climate activism's political impotence' and soothing the masses with 'a false sense of hope'. There is no way a movement can ever get its hands on fossil fuel combustion. 'No matter how many people take to the streets in massive marches or in direct actions', the energy is beyond reach, because people 'do not help produce it. They only consume.' One should think that the movement has refuted this quitter talk by now, but Scranton has sustained it deep into the third cycle. In an essay published in the *Los Angeles Review of Books* in June 2019, he takes McKibben and David Wallace-Wells, author of *The Uninhabitable Earth*, to task for suggesting that action might still avert the worst-case scenarios and announces that 'only the deluded and naïve could maintain that non-violent protest politics is much more than ritualized wishful thinking'. What else, then, should be done? For one brief moment, Scranton seems to flirt with the idea of transcending pacifism – 'the real reason that non-violence is considered to be a virtue in the powerless is that the powerful do not want to see their lives or property threatened' – only to come down firmly against *any* action.

Instead we should cross our legs in a lotus position and think. On the way down, Buddhist meditation can give us peace of mind. 'If the bad news we must confront is that we're all gonna die, then the wisdom that might help us deal with that news arises from the realisation that it was going to happen anyway.' If the self can only understand that 'it was already dying, already dead', then it can crash to the bottom with equanimity; if it can also understand that everything around it is fleeting and insubstantial – a speck of dust in the cosmos, to be blown away in a milli-second – it can quietly let go of the world. It won't hurt much. Activists have so far hankered for the world to be saved; the point, however, is to accept its end. The highest stage of consciousness is 'willing our fate', and action blocks the way to such ataraxy. 'With every protest chant', Scranton bemoans, 'we become weaker thinkers.' We should rather cultivate 'detachment', suspend 'our partici-pation in social life' and accommodate 'our souls to death'.

How can this message find resonance with a reading audience in the North? Most probably because it offers one articulation of the despair business-as-usual foments in the breakdown. For Scranton, however, everything begins with himself. He is an introspective and self-reveal-ing essayist, the species of writer who feels that his readers need to know that he once had 'a torrid affair with a German woman ten years my senior who flew me to stay with her in Hamburg' and builds a political worldview on that kind of data. A sense of personal failure underlines his sentences. 'I'm a bad environmentalist', he writes, by which he means that he cannot control his own acts of pollution. Scranton drives for hours on end, flies 'all the time', throws cups away, binges on beef and tuna from 'the worst places'. 'I know it's wrong, but I do it anyway.' Scranton treats himself as a source of information about the alterability of the ruling order. The odds are zero that 'I, personally, will ever be able to do anything to stop or even slow down global climate change', and it follows that 'you're heating up the planet. We do it every day. We can't stop. We won't stop.' Presumably a white man who can't stop using the N-word for black people while seeing his own face in the mirror of the world would be unable to envision racism rooted out of society. On the climate question, this attitude breeds the certainty 'that the problem is us' – struggle would be possible if an enemy could be identified, but 'global warming offers no apprehensible foe', no one to fight, only the ceaselessly sinning culprit that is 'ourselves'. And since this self cannot even bring himself to put the paper cups in the right bin, doomed we are.

Like all individuals, Scranton has a political trajectory, and it has crossed paths with collective action at several points. As a young man in Oregon, he participated in a campaign against a petroleum pipeline across the Cascade mountains; the campaign prevailed, the pipeline wasn't built, and still the experience left him with a bitter taste of vanity. He marched against WTO on the streets of Seattle in 1999 and thereby lost 'what faith I had left in protest-based social movements', a rather idiosyncratic reaction to that episode (another young demonstrator was so enraptured that it stayed in his vision as he became one of the key organisers of Ende Gelände). 'I was done with eco-warriors, tree huggers, and anarchists; I wanted nothing to do at all with the politics of our fallen world.' And so Scranton took the step into what is plainly his most formative political experience: he joined the US army. He signed up for Iraq. He was so disillusioned by the left, so shaken by 9/11, so swayed by hawks like Christopher Hitchens and convinced of the need to crush Islamic terrorism that he burned with desire to do 'the dirty work of empire'. He also wished to become a man and clear up his 'deep insecurity about my masculinity'. He hungered for action.

In the beginning, he loved it; part of him still seems to. 'Those brutal, maddening days in Baghdad in the summer of 2003', Scranton writes in a book published sixteen years later, 'were some of the sweetest and purest of my life. Each moment gleamed with a transcendent splendor.' He recalls moments 'sweeter than sex, the gut-grinning crunch of ramming a civilian car, angels singing as I sped through jammed intersections without stopping, God's own righteousness when I picked up my rifle to take a man in my sights'. He retains some pride in his service: 'We kept Iraqi kids from blowing themselves up and denied insurgents weapons.' But eventually, a sense of rot set in. Scranton lost his faith in the occupation too. He had to give up 'the fragile illusion that we might have done some good in Iraq' and come full-circle to the insight that the American mistakes were not accidental, but part of 'a consistent pattern of imperialist manipulation' in the

Middle East. The whole war was a 'crooked enterprise' and 'I had profited by it. I had let it happen, and I had made it happen.' Since then, Scranton appears to have regarded the world through a sniper scope that curves back on himself and made this the basis of a public profile on climate change. In his essays, the climate is homologous with Iraq: an unmitigated catastrophe that *I* helped create, a blunder impossible to get out of, a tragic show of the folly of human action, which tends to have terrible, irreversible consequences. Mitigating global heating, Scranton deduces, is as unfeasible as resurrecting the children killed under the command of George W. Bush.

An enduring commitment to resistance would yield a different position on climate. A conflicted soul and intellect, Scranton cannot fully hold back the radical spasms of his youth – he occasionally lashes out against capitalism; towards the end of *We're Doomed*, he even calls for 'socialist revolution' and places it within the realm of the possible, given enough 'dedicated cadres' – but when the lights go out, he reaches for his Stoics and his Buddha. Resignation before the inevitable is his main credo.

If this were a mere personal quirk, it would merit no comment, but Scranton shares this position with inter alia Jonathan Franzen, a rather more senior member of the American literary pantheon. From his pulpit in the *New Yorker*, he has periodically held forth on how unwise it is to attempt to have climate change abated. Like Scranton, he believes that 'planetary overheating is a done deal'. As his evidence, he points to the fact that 'no head of state has ever made a commitment to leaving any carbon in the ground'. Before the 1790s, no head of a state had ever made a commitment to freeing African slaves; in July 1791, someone of Franzen's disposition could have argued, on these grounds alone, that eternal slavery is a done deal. For the novelist, the fact that emissions have continued to rise over the past three decades proves that they cannot be cut – a non sequitur every struggle in a time of exasperation has had to shake off. He admits that the lack of progress so far admits of two options: you can feel ever more 'enraged by the world's inaction. Or you can accept that disaster is coming', and he would not advise feeling the rage.

Franzen, like Scranton, feels guilty about his ungovernable driving and flying. He distrusts his own ability to cut back on combustion or contribute to the wider endeavour. But this culpability is in the nature of the species: 'human beings are killers of the natural world'; 'we'll all be sinners in the hands of an angry Earth'. And this human nature is not going to change (Franzen includes in it things like 'nationalism and class and racial resentments' that obstruct mitigation.) Finding himself in such a cul-de-sac, 'what makes intuitive moral sense' to the novelist is '*to live the life I was given*' – that is, to go on living the life of a prosperous American intellectual. Franzen professes awareness of the dimensions of the climate catastrophe, as does Scranton, who believes it is 'bigger than World War II, bigger than racism, sexism, inequality, slavery, the Holocaust, the end of nature, the

Sixth Extinction, famine, war, and plague *all put together*', a vertiginous bigness that renders surrender prudent and mandatory. Scranton is sceptical about renewable energy expansion (he thinks it will be too expensive and intermittent), Franzen hostile (he fears it will kill his beloved birds). Both men favour adaptation. We can adapt, Franzen argues, more sanguine than his companion – we humans have always been 'brilliant adapters; climate change is just the same old story writ larger'. Personal advice from the great American novelist: like me, go on living the life you were given, to the best of your ability.

One might think that this position – call it climate fatalism – belongs to a certain type of American intelligentsia looking out over a planet above 400 ppm. But that would be incorrect. It is older and wider than that. After COP15, novelist Paul Kingsnorth bit off a chunk of the British climate movement for the Dark Mountain Project, whose core tenets were and remain that the unravelling of civilisation is unstoppable, that the ecological crisis is uncontainable and that collective action against either is a wild-goose chase. He found a Swedish disciple in David Jonstad, a notable intellectual of the first-cycle direct action groups, who now asseverated that it was all over and retreated into the countryside to establish a farm for himself and his family and learn to hunt. He wrote his first book on carbon rationing as a solution to the crisis, his second on the inevitability of collapse, his third on the virtues of a self-sufficient household. The paths to cave-in are many.

What appears to unite them, at least on the surface, is a reification of despair. The latter is an eminently understandable emotional response to the crisis, but unserviceable as a foundation for a politics in it. As another climate philosopher, Catriona McKinnon, has argued in the article 'Climate Change: Against Despair', a delightful logical evisceration of the fatalist position, it often comes down to a probability assessment. While some climate fatalists deny that it would be logically and technically possible to cut emissions to zero and then begin the work of repair and regeneration, more common is the argument that this just won't happen, because of the way the world is. Scranton at one point acknowledges that it *could* be accomplished, if we managed to 'radically reorient all human economic and social production, a task that is *scarcely imaginable*, much less feasible. It would demand centralized control of key economic sectors, massive state investment in carbon capture and sequestration, and global coordination on a scale never seen before' – a scenario that can be conjured up in some theoretical hemisphere of the mind but not promoted or implemented in the real world, because the forces stacked against it are so stupefyingly strong. Despair about the climate is here based on a judgement of extreme improbability, hypostatised into impossibility. The procedure is anti-political through and through.

If someone seeks to affect the ways of the world by acting in one way rather than another, it must be because she holds an outcome to be desirable and wants to contribute to its realisation. If she merely wished to confirm the most probable outcome *on account of its high probability*, she would have no reason to act at all. Her behaviour would have no normative substance. It would have no strategic charge. She would simply be floating, and she would be floating just for the sake of it. To act politically is to reject probability assessment as a ground for action (since it could inspire no action), and this applies to men like Scranton and Franzen too: through their writings, they seek to influence others to do one thing over another. Else they would keep their mouths shut. If Scranton believed that people would take up the lotus position in the fall down the chasm with the same probability as a bird spreading its wings, his recommendations would be redundant. Climate fatalism is a performative contradiction. It does not passively reflect a certain distribution of probabilities but *actively affirms it* – or, with McKinnon, 'it may become a self-fulfilling prophecy: that which is repeatedly asserted to be impossible can thereby become impossible'. The more people who tell us that a radical reorientation is 'scarcely imaginable', the less imaginable it will be.

Imagination is a pivotal faculty here. The climate crisis unfolds through a series of interlocked absurdities ingrained in it: not only is it easier to imagine the end of the world than the end of capitalism, or the deliberate, large-scale intervention in the climate system – what we refer to as geoengineering – than in the economic system; it is also easier, at least for some, to imagine learning to die than learning to fight, to reconcile oneself to the end of everything one holds dear than to consider some militant resistance. Climate fatalism does all in its power to confirm these paralysing absurdities. Indeed, that is its vocation. If it rests on personal shortcomings, it becomes no less absurd; as McKinnon shows, if an individual cannot muster the will to reduce his own emissions, this in itself does not establish that he is unable to do so. Roy Scranton may not have a motivation sufficient to pick a different dish from the menu than the bloodiest steak, but *he could do it*, in the sense that if he were to try 'and not give up' – the crucial proviso – he would 'tend to succeed'. What despair here amounts to is that 'I can make no difference because I am unwilling to make a difference'. The same goes, of course, for every perpetrator of luxury emissions. A climate fatalist of the Scranton–Franzen type (the self-sufficient hunter-farmer is a separate case) then projects this weakness of the flesh onto society, elevating the individual inability to change the established order to a universal fact. It is easier to imagine the end of the world than me skipping a filet mignon.

The fatalist might counter that doubts about personal emissions reductions pertain not to their possibility as such, but to their effects. My foregoing that steak would have not one iota of impact on an atmosphere staggering under billions of gigatons of carbon. This, however, McKinnon points out, is but a version of the sorites paradox: if one grain of sand is removed from a heap, this will not destroy the heap; if one identical grain is removed, the heap is still there, and so on and so forth, until nothing is left. Translated to the climate: my flight today between London and New York makes no difference to cumulative emissions; therefore, neither did the same flight I took last week; if this is true of my flights, then it must be true of everyone else's flights and other acts of emission, and so we end up with the conclusion that *climate change is not anthropogenic.* Or, consider a hypothetical case of torture. Someone is wired to a torture machine with 1,000 switches, each identical to the next. When no switch is flipped, there is no current in the machine and the victim feels nothing; when all are flipped, she screams in unbearable pain. Between 0 and 1,000, very many switches can be flipped, each in itself of tiny consequence, adding up to a current that must at some point cross the threshold of pain. Transferred to the climate: the first ever act of emission made no difference, similarly for the second, and so on, 'until we reach a point at which the climate has clearly changed'. Somewhere along the way – if the problem is anthropogenic – at least one act of emission must have made a perceptible difference, and the same must then apply to a reversal of the sequence.

Now McKinnon works in the best tradition of liberal political philosophy, and so she focuses precisely on *individual* emissions, but the logic could be converted to the central force field of collective action. If we accept that climate change is the cumulative effect of action at the level of class – the product of fossil capital and the classes ruling on its behalf – then every time the switch is flipped, a counteraction could, logically, in principle, negate that action and turn the switch off. If the collective supplying the counterforce were to try and not give up, it might succeed (logically speaking, still). This must have held throughout the history of CO_2 emissions. But maybe it is now too late? What if we have reached, say, 666 on the switch panel and the machine is so constructed that there is no going back from this point, only forward towards maximum pain? This is the putatively scientific case for climate fatalism: because so much has been already emitted, what cuts we make now and henceforth will make too little difference to justify the herculean effort involved. Problem is that this case has no basis in the science. 'It is not a question of whether we can limit warming but whether we choose to do so', runs a standard phrase from the peer-reviewed literature on the state of the climate as we enter the 2020s ('we' here meaning humanity, which divides itself into antagonistic blocs). 'The precise level of future warming', Tong and his colleagues make clear, 'depends largely on infrastructure that has not yet been built.' It *could* be blocked.

The alpha and omega of the science of the cumulative character of climate change run contrary to the axioms of fatalism. *Every gigaton matters*, every single plant and terminal and pipeline and SUV and superyacht makes a difference to the aggregate damage done, and this is just as true above 400 ppm and 1°C as it is below. It won't lose its truth at 500 ppm or 2°C or higher still. The totality of global heating will always be a function of the totality of emissions – less of the latter, less of the former. Positive feedback mechanisms do not cancel out this function, only beef it up. Wallace-Wells has the science behind him when he writes: 'The fight is, definitely, not yet lost – in fact will never be lost, so long as we avoid extinction, because however warm the planet gets, it will always be the case that the decade that follows could contain more suffering or less.' If fatalists think that mitigation is meaningful only at a time when damage is yet to be done, they have misunderstood the basics of both climate science and movement.

Nowhere is the latter so naïve as to think that global heating as such could still be averted. It gets its urgency and rage from the knowledge that it is happening, that too much damage has already been done already – as expressed in the very names of the groups: 350.org, Extinction Rebellion, Ende Gelände – and that no efforts should now be spared in preventing even more of it. The movement knows that it faces a giant salvaging operation: safeguarding as much space as possible on this scarred planet for human and other life to survive and maybe thrive and, in the best case, healing some of the wounds from the past centuries. A demand such as the prohibition of all new CO_2-emitting devices loses none of its relevance at higher concentrations and temperatures, but precisely the opposite; the later in the day, the more imperative to enforce it by any means necessary. Overshoot of targets for climate mitigation calls for more, not less, resistance. This extends to geoengineering scenarios – the onset of solar radiation management, the roll-out of negative emissions technologies – which would rapidly fall apart without concomitant closure of CO_2 sources. Until business-as-usual is a distant memory, as long as humans are around, resistance is the path to survival in all weathers; it didn't become passé in 2009 and it won't do so in 2029.

No one knows exactly how this crisis will end. No scientist, no activist, no novelist, no modeller or soothsayer knows it, because too many variables of human action determine the outcome. If collectives throw themselves against the switches with sufficient force, there will be no more flipping towards peak torture; the pain might be ameliorated. Within these parameters, one acts or one does not. Like each grain of sand in the pile, an individual joining the counter-collective could boost its capacity on the margin, and the counter-collective could get the better of the enemy. No more is required to maintain a minimum of hope: success is neither certain nor probable, but *possible*. 'The context for hope is radical uncertainty', writes McKinnon; 'anything could happen, and whether we act or not has everything to do with it', Rebecca Solnit. 'Hope is not a door, but a sense that there might be a door somewhere.' Or, more poignantly still, 'hope is an axe you break down doors with in an emergency'.

People wielding that axe have always been told that we're fucked, we're doomed, we should just try to scrape by, nothing will ever change for the better; from the slave barracks to the Judenräte and onwards, every revolt has been discouraged by the elders of defeatism. But what of the revolts that actually failed? Did they not validate the naysayers? What was the point of Nat Turner or the Warsaw ghetto uprising? Fatalism of the present holds defeated struggles of the past in contempt, and so does strategic pacifism: if someone raised a weapon and lost, it was because she raised that weapon. She shouldn't have. Chenoweth and Stephan chide the Palestinians for using rocks and petrol bombs in the first intifada; had they only managed to stay peaceful – had the leadership been able to 'convince youths to stop throwing rocks' – they would have won the West Bank and the Gaza Strip. Such arrogance may be bred from within the ivory and concrete towers of the empire. (Adding to the ironies of pacifism, Maria Stephan composed her portion of *Why Civil Resistance Works* from the US embassy in Kabul. She was a lead officer in the state department's Bureau of Conflict and Stabilization Operations, whose mission is 'to anticipate, prevent, and respond to conflict that undermines U.S. national interests'. As of this writing, the Bureau's website displays the picture of masked youth building barricades and throwing Molotov cocktails.)

Likewise, Chenoweth and Stephan castigate the Fedaiyan for continuing the fight against Ayatollah Khomeini: the post-1979 guerrilla campaigns merely served the regime with 'a pretext for purging' Iranian society of unwanted elements. In the universe of strategic pacifism, only the winners deserve praise. (But I should perhaps acknowledge a personal bias of my own here: a close family member was a leading militant of the

Fedaiyan. She was tortured as a teenager in the dungeons of the Shah, smuggled weapons and coordinated underground cells under the Ayatollah and, after the final defeat, washed up in Sweden a wreck.)

Disparagement of the defeated can be reframed in terms of just war theory: resistance, including armed self-defence, is justified only if it is *likely* to stave off the threat. A victim has no right to fight back if she is doomed in advance. But this 'success condition' has objectionable consequences, regarding, for instance, the Warsaw ghetto uprising. The Jews who scraped together what guns they could find knew for certain that they would be crushed by the Nazis and, just as expected, achieved nothing in military terms. So should they have let themselves been supinely ferried off to Treblinka and Auschwitz? The case can, *mutatis mutandis*, be transposed to the climate. Imagine that it *really is* too late. We're over the cliff. Apocalyptic heating is a done deal, no matter what. Scranton and Franzen have no scientific substantiation for the claim that this is the case now, and it would probably take some time for it to come to pass, but it cannot be ruled out entirely: one can imagine a hothouse Earth scenario, where positive feedback mechanisms drive the planet into an orbit of uncontrollable heating. Surely it must *then* be pointless to resist?

Imagine that diminished human populations eke out an existence near the poles. They will be around for a couple of more decades. Some of their offspring might have a chance to hold on a little longer. What would we want to tell them? That humanity brought about the end of the world in perfect harmony? That everyone willingly queued up for the furnaces? Or that some people fought like Jews who knew they would be killed?

> In the ghettos, as in the extermination camps to which they were the antechamber, the *résistants* embarked on a race against death. To struggle and resist was the only lucid choice, but this most often meant for the fighters no more than choosing the time and manner of their death. Beyond the immediate outcome of the struggle, which most often was inevitable, their combat was for history, for memory . . . *This affirmation of life by way of a sacrifice and combat with no prospect of victory* is a tragic paradox that can only be understood as an act of faith in history,

Alain Brossat and Sylvie Klingberg write in *Revolutionary Yiddishland*. Precisely the hopelessness of the situation constituted the nobility of this resistance. The rebels affirmed life so extraordinarily robustly because death was certain and *still* they fought on. It can never, ever be too late for that gesture. If it is too late for resistance to be waged within a calculus of immediate utility, the time has come for it to vindicate the fundamental values of life, even if it only means crying out to the heavens. To make that statement would require some forceful type of action. This is the moment for the cliché from Emiliano Zapata:

'It is better to die on your feet than to live on your knees'
– better to die blowing up a pipeline than to burn impas-
sively – but we shall hope, of course, that it never comes
to this. If we resist fatalism, it might not. The research that
does suggest that some tipping points might have already
been crossed – such as, notably, the melting of the West
Antarctic ice sheet – only underscores the need for emergency tactics; if more points are crossed, that need rises
further still, until, in the worst case, the time comes for
Warsaw.

In the less eschatological conjuncture we still live in,
we would be better served by honouring past struggles
– including those defeated – than sneering at them,
because it would prime us for staying on their path. Defeat
also has a pedagogical function, including for the climate
movement: without COP15 and the disappointments of
early Obama, there might have been no turn towards mass
action. Climate fatalism is for the jaded and the deflated;
it is a 'bourgeois luxury', in the plain language of one
Swedish critic. In a memorable section of *We're Doomed*,
Scranton enjoys a conversation with Timothy Morton,
another acclaimed writer and compulsive luxury emitter.
Morton illuminates for Scranton how the climate catastrophe is an epiphany of 'OMG, I am the destruction. I'm
part of it and I'm in it and I'm on it. It's an aesthetic experience, I'm inside it, I'm involved, I'm implicated.' The
trick is to find enjoyment in this moment. 'I think that's
how we get to smile, eventually, by fully inhabiting catastrophe space, in the same way that eventually a nightmare

can become so horrible that you start laughing.' You won't hear anything like this in Dominica. You won't hear poor people who today *actually* are at risk of dying in the catastrophe – in the Philippines, in Mozambique, in Peru – say, 'I am the destruction. It's an aesthetic experience. I may as well laugh at it.' Where climate death is a reality, not philosophical chic, programmatic fatalism of the Scranton–Franzen school has zero traction (religious fatalism is another matter). Nor can the guilt that animates it be found on the vulnerable peripheries. Nor can the trust in self-reliant adaptation.

Climate fatalism is for those on top; its sole contribution is spoilage. The most religiously Gandhian climate activist, the most starry-eyed renewable energy entrepreneur, the most self-righteous believer in veganism as panacea, the most compromise-prone parliamentarian is infinitely preferable to the white man of the North who says, 'We're doomed – fall in peace.' Within the range of positions this side of climate denial, none is more despicable.

A reader well versed in the history of Northern environmentalism will by now have asked: then what about the ecologists who practised sabotage on some scale from the 1980s to the early 2000s? Those were the days of Earth First!, Animal Liberation Front and Earth Liberation Front. Their campaigns of 'monkeywrenching' or 'ecotage' prospered in a certain subculture that reached its apogee in the 1990s, mingling punk and hardcore with dumpster

groupuscules and individuals pulled off a global grand total of 27,100 actions between 1973 and 2010, painstakingly recorded by the main scholarly authority, Michael Loadenthal. The largest portion defaced property by spraying graffiti – another form of low-key sabotage left outside the arsenal of the climate movement – but tyres were also slashed, vehicles burnt, windows smashed, locks glued, trees spiked, bombs and noise bombs and sound bombs thrown, the list manifesting some rather vivid imagination. Targets were chosen promiscuously. Ecotage hit McDonalds restaurants, banks, GMO research offices, fur retailers, mink farms (those were the days of thousands of minks 'liberated' into American and Swedish forests), hunting lodges, a wildlife museum – activists burning down exhibitions of stuffed animals – ranches, hatcheries, apartment construction sites, a ski resort encroaching on a lynx habitat and sundry other objects. In 1996, ELF glued the locks on a Chevron petrol station in Eugene, Oregon. In 1998, explosions tore through equipment for oil and gas extraction in Alberta, Canada. In 2003, ELF cells claimed responsibility for attacks on four car dealers in the San Gabriel Valley in southern California; one car lot storing new SUVs lost forty Hummers to the flames (the *Los Angeles Times* had the discernment to report this as 'vandalism', not terrorism). That was one of the last high-profile actions of the submovement, which petered out just as the climate movement came into its own.

What can be gleaned from this interlude? Loadenthal highlights the fact that the 27,100 actions caused exactly four fatalities, all of them at the hands of attackers unaffiliated to any group (namely, the Unabomber and the man who assassinated the Dutch politician Pim Fortuyn). EF!, ALF and ELF never killed anyone. 99.9 per cent of their actions caused zero injury. This was, of course, a deliberate choice: 'Houses were checked for all forms of life, and we even moved a propane tank out of the house all the way across the street just because – in [the] worst case scenario – the firefighters could get hurt', said a typical ELF communiqué. This might be the most compelling evidence so far for the possibility of property destruction without violence against people. It would seem to provide yet more contrast to Lanchester's paradox – if all of this happened so recently, why so little of it now? But the paradox might, from another viewpoint, rather have a straightforward solution: the climate movement took off *because* it had no connections to the ecosystem of EF!, ALF and ELF. Had it started with ecotage, it would have gone nowhere. All those thousands of monkeywrenching actions achieved little if anything and had no lasting gains to show for them. They were not performed in a dynamic relation to a mass movement, but largely in a void.

The limited use-value of this history is fully borne out in *Deep Green Resistance*. Its authors are sworn to pure substitutionism: small nuclei of military combatants file out of their bunkers in lieu of the masses. 'It is our prediction that there will be no mass movement' – 'are you willing to set aside your last, fierce dream of that brave uprising of millions strong?' This is despair, disproven on the issue of the climate, masquerading as militancy. Or, if you will, the incompatibility thesis of strategic pacifism with the signs reversed: no masses, only the armed vanguard. McBay and his colleagues are unabashed elitists. It is enough to recruit one out of 100,000 persons, as long as the 'warriors' are of a spotless character – 'better to have a reliable few than an unstable more'. These valiant few have the mission to undo human civilisation as it has developed since the ice age. Like the quondam praxis of ecotage, *Deep Green Resistance* casts its net as wide as the enemy is hazy: the attacks shall target bridges, tunnels, mountain passes, dams, factories, the electrical grid, the internet – Jensen has also proposed 'immediately taking down every cell phone tower in the world' – banks and the Bombay Stock Exchange, in addition to the power plants and the pipelines.

The last 300 pages of *Deep Green Resistance* serve as a manual on something called 'Decisive Ecological Warfare'. The aim is to 'induce widespread industrial collapse, beyond any economic or political systems' – to reduce organised human life to a *tabula rasa* and hand the planet back to the animal kingdom. A few years of war will be enough for the roving commandos to cut CO_2 emissions by 90 per cent. Presumably there will also be some population reduction along the way. Murder is no longer abhorred – 'uniquely valuable individuals make uniquely valuable targets for assassination' – as the deep-green guerrillas fight their way through the continents, wade through rising rivers of blood and collect firewood for surviving elders, in a book of revelation whose climactic battles bring to mind *The Turner Diaries* and other American fantasies of race war. It is another ending for deep ecology. It makes the very notion of violent resistance appear nauseating.

Perhaps the climate movement has, after all, learned the lesson well by not even considering going down this route. Less than a map for troop movements, *Deep Green Resistance* should be read as a symptom of hardening despair and deadlock. Perhaps there will be more fever dreams of this kind on a burning planet. Perhaps every instance of toying with the idea of violence is part of the syndrome. Sanity has been robbed from us.

How could a militant climate struggle avoid veering down into such deep ditches? The set-up would, for a start, inverse deep ecology: whereas the latter wants to wage war against civilisation and indeed humanity as such, the former would fight for the *possibility* of civilisation, in the sense of organised social life for Homo sapiens. Unlike the deep variety, it would target a particular deformed kind of civilisation – namely, that erected on the plinth of fossil capital – and tear it down so that another form of civilisation can endure (or none will). This implies that climate militancy would have to be articulated to a wider anti-capitalist groundswell, much as in earlier shifts of modes of production, when physical attacks on ruling classes formed only minor parts of society-wide reorganisation. How could that happen? This cannot be known beforehand. It can be found out only through immersion in practice.

Ende Gelände in 2016 targeted the mine and railway tracks around Schwarze Pumpe, 'the black pump', an enormous power plant in the eastern region of Lusatia running on brown coal and belching out volcanic columns of smoke from concave chimneys. Fuel is conveyed from the nearby mega-mine via railway tracks. Up until the year of the action, Schwarze Pumpe and four similar facilities in Germany had been the property of Vattenfall, an energy corporation owned by the Swedish state and subject to directives from its government. In the Swedish parliamentary elections of 2014, Gustav Fridolin, leader of the Greens, kept a lump of coal in his pocket. Wherever he went, in every speech and televised debate, he waved that lump and promised, stern determination in his voice, to put a lid on the coal in the ground. Vattenfall's brown coal complexes in Germany produced CO_2 emissions equal to the total from Swedish territory plus a third; no single measure would cut emissions as radically as their closure. Fridolin and the Greens pledged themselves to it if they entered government. They entered government, and two years later, Schwarze Pumpe and its four sister facilities were slated to be out of Swedish possession. They were going to be *sold* to a consortium of capitalists from the Czech Republic – including its richest man – craving more resources for the brown coal renaissance in which they invested. The Swedish state, governed by social democrats and greens, had resolved not to close some of the greatest coal riches of the continent, but to throw them straight into the jaws of fossil capital.

Up on the railway tracks, no wagons running, the blockade in full effect, my affinity group itched for more. We wanted to press on. So did hundreds of others in white coveralls, holding impromptu assemblies and banding together for a manoeuvre not planned in advance and not covered by the action consensus. We marched away from the tracks, towards the power plant itself. In the patch of forest surrounding it, we encountered a fence. Walking, half-running in the front, my affinity group tore it down, broke it apart, stamped on it and continued with the rest of the march up to the perimeters of the plant. They were marked by another, sturdier fence, also pulled down. The few private guards caught off-hand and completely outnumbered, we rushed into the compound. During my years in the climate movement, I have never felt a greater rush of exhilaration: for one throbbing, mind-expanding moment, we had a slice of the infrastructure wrecking this planet in our hands. We could do with it as we wanted. We streamed through the area, as amazed as the guards that we had entered and with no plans for how to proceed; we checked some gates here, entered a tower there, sprayed a slogan in a corner, unsure of how to complete the shut-down, until police forces arrived and chased us away with their batons and spray. We returned to the encircling belt of blockades. The morning after, Vattenfall declared that Ende Gelände had enforced the suspension of all electricity production, something that had never before happened at a fossil-fuelled power plant in Europe.

The corporation, media, politicians were aghast. 'It's a completely new phenomenon when violent pressure is used to shut off production and directly intervene in the German energy system', said the CEO of Vattenfall's continental operations. He complained of a 'trail of devastation' and referred to the destruction of the fences as *massiven kriminellen Gewalttaten*, 'massive criminal violence'. This phrase was repeated by the mayor of the town, who declared that 'you cannot imagine any worse damage than what these people did. One of the main arguments for this region and for the Schwarze Pumpe industrial park is: we are industry-friendly. This nullifies the image we try to establish with investors.' (Less than a year later, the new Czech owners shelved their plans for expanding the mine serving Schwarze Pumpe and another pit, citing adverse political developments; Ende Gelände claimed partial victory.) Civil disobedience comes to an end 'when things are destroyed', one public broadcaster denounced the action. Gustav Fridolin branded it 'illegal'.

The incident of the stormed compound took on a life of its own, as a sign of the purportedly violent nature of Ende Gelände in eastern Germany. It brought home more absurdities of the situation: the breaking of fences could be officially framed as *massiven kriminellen Gewalttaten*, devastation, unimaginable damage, whereas the perpetual cloud of CO_2 from Schwarze Pumpe was the mark of a peaceful normality. This warping had something to do with the political conjuncture in those eastern districts, where the Alternative für Deutschland (AfD) – the far-right party that denies climate, loves coal and wants the bottom of the German mines to be scraped – has its main bastions of support. No one was more incensed about the incursion than the AfD. In the hours after it, a mob of far-right activists and locals assaulted several of the Ende Gelände blockades, shooting firecrackers into them and chasing activists in cars. More violence of that kind should perhaps be anticipated, as the task of defending fossil capital is passed on to the far right in Europe and elsewhere.

But if destroying fences was an act of violence, it was violence of the sweetest kind. I was high for weeks afterwards. All the despair that climate breakdown generates on a daily basis was out of my system, if only temporarily; I had had an injection of collective empowerment. There is a famous line in *The Wretched of the Earth* where Frantz Fanon writes of violence as a 'cleansing force'. It frees the native 'from his despair and inaction; it makes him fearless and restores his self-respect'. Few processes produce as much despair as global heating. Imagine that, someday, the reservoirs of that emotion built up around the world – in the global South in particular – find their outlets. There has been a time for a Gandhian climate movement; perhaps there might come a time for a Fanonian one. The breaking of fences may one day be seen as a very minor misdemeanour indeed.

Notes

p. 6. **Since then, total annual CO₂ emissions ...** Emissions figures calculated from Tom Boden, Bob Andres and Gregg Marland, 'Global CO₂ Emissions from Fossil-Fuel Burning, Cement Manufacture, and Gas Flaring: 1751–2014', Carbon Dioxide Information Analysis Center, cdiac.essdive.lbl.gov, 3 March 2017; Corinne Le Quéré, Robbie M. Andrew, Pierre Friedlingstein et al., 'Global Carbon Budget 2018', *Earth System Science Data* 10 (2018): 2141–94. The years 2019 and 2020 are included in the estimate of emissions made in the twenty-five years after COP1, using the conservative (unrealistically so) assumption that emissions during these years would remain at the level of 2018.

p. 7. **Since COP1, the US has set off a boom ...** Figures on pipeline mileage from Bureau of Transportation Statistics, 'U.S. Oil and Gas Pipeline Mileage', bts.gov, 28 March 2019; American Petroleum Institute, *Pipeline 101*, pipeline101.org, 2016 (accessed 28 August 2019).

p. 7. **In April 1995, the month . . .** Atmospheric concentration of CO_2 as measured at the Mauna Loa Observatory and reported by the National Oceanic and Atmospheric Administration, published at *CO$_2$ Earth*, co2.earth (accessed 28 August 2019).

p. 7. **A cloud of smoke . . .** Jonathan Watts, 'Arctic Wildfires Spew Soot and Smoke Cloud Bigger than EU', *Guardian*, theguardian.com, 12 August 2019.

p. 9. **In the summer of 2017, the Gulf of Mexico . . .** Kevin E. Trenberth, Lijing Cheng, Peter Jacobs et al., 'Hurricane Harvey Links to Ocean Heat Content and Climate Change Adaptation', *Earth's Future* 6 (2018): 730–44.

p. 9. **It tore through the Caribbean island of Dominica . . .** See e.g. Patrick Cloos and Valéry Ridde, 'Research on Climate Change, Health Inequities, and Migration in the Caribbean', *Lancet* 2 (2018): 4–5.

p. 9. **Skerrit spoke of himself . . .** Skerrit's speech can be watched on YouTube: 'PM Roosevelt Skerrit of Dominica Speech to the General Assembly at the United Nations 2017', uploaded 23 September 2017. The official transcript can be found at *UN News*, ' "To Deny Climate Change Is to Deny a Truth We Have Just Lived", Says Prime Minister of Storm-Hit Dominica', news.un.org, 23 September 2017.

p. 10. **The government put the death toll . . .** On Hurricane Maria in Puerto Rico and the various mortality estimates, see e.g. David Keellings and José J. Hernández Ayala, 'Extreme Rainfall Associated with Hurricane Maria over Puerto Rico and Its Connections to Climate Change',

Geophysical Research Letters 46 (2019): 2964–73; Nishant Kishore, Domingo Marqués, Ayesha Mahmud et al., 'Mortality in Puerto Rico after Hurricane Maria', *New England Journal of Medicine* 379 (2018): 162–70; Carlos Santos-Burgoa, John Sandberg, Erick Suárez et al., 'Differential and Persistent Risk of Excess Mortality from Hurricane Maria in Puerto Rico: A Time-Series Analysis', *Lancet Planet Health* 2 (2018): 478–88.

p. 11. **'It is strange and striking ...'** John Lanchester, 'Warmer, Warmer', *London Review of Books* 29, no. 6 (2007), p. 3.

p. 13. **The climate movement in the global North ...** Useful accounts of the evolution of the movement include Matthias Dietz and Heiko Garrelts (eds.), *Routledge Handbook of the Climate Change Movement* (Abingdon, UK: Routledge, 2014); Carl Cassegård, Linda Soneryd, Håkan Thörn and Åsa Wettergren (eds.), *Climate Action in a Globalizing World: Comparative Perspectives on Environmental Movements in the Global North* (New York: Routledge, 2017); Andrew Cheon and Johannes Urpelainen, *Activism and the Fossil Fuel Industry* (Abingdon, UK: Routledge, 2018), the latter with an exclusive focus on the US movement.

p. 17. **according to a newly released report ...** Sveriges Kommuner och Landsting, *Klimatförändringarnas lokala effekter: Exempel från tre kommuner*, skr.se, June 2019.

p. 19. **'If the emissions have to stop ...'** Greta Thunberg, *No One Is Too Small to Make a Difference* (London: Penguin, 2018), pp. 7, 10.

p. 19. **'How dare you! . . .'** Greta Thunberg, 'If World Leaders Choose to Fail Us, My Generation Will Never Forgive Them', *Guardian*, 23 September 2019.

p. 19. **Back home in Sweden, one of them . . .** Maria G. Francke, 'En ny Greta är född', *Sydsvenska Dagbladet*, sydsvenskan.se, 23 September 2019.

p. 20. **At Ende Gelände, activists pitch . . .** Despite its weight, Ende Gelände has, at the moment of this writing, been conspicuous by its absence in anglophone scholarship on the movement. One exception is Leah Temper, 'Radical Climate Politics: From Ogoniland to Ende Gelände', in Ruth Kinna and Uri Gordon (eds.), *Routledge Handbook of Radical Politics* (New York: Routledge, 2019), pp. 97–106.

p. 26. **In May 2019, just weeks . . .** International Energy Agency, *World Energy Investment 2019*, iea.org/wei2019. Quotations on new pipelines from p. 105. The profit measure used for ExxonMobil is 'internal rate of return' (p. 89).

p. 27. **despite the latter now being 'consistently cheaper' . . .** Dominic Dudley, 'Renewable Energy Costs Take Another Tumble, Making Fossil Fuels Look More Expensive Than Ever', *Forbes*, forbes.com, 29 May 2019.

p. 27. **'a growing mismatch' . . .** International Energy Agency, 'Global Energy Investment Stabilised above USD 1.8 Trillion in 2018, but Security and Sustainability Concerns Are Growing', iea.org, 14 May 2019.

p. 27. **The world's fifty largest oil companies . . .** Jonathan Watts, Jillian Ambrose and Adam Vaughan, 'Oil Firms to Pour Extra 7m Barrels per Day into Markets, Data Shows', *Guardian*, 10 October 2019.

p. 27. **as the *Guardian* also revealed . . .** Patrick Greenfield, 'World's Top Three Asset Managers Oversee $300bn Fossil Fuel Investments', *Guardian*, 12 October 2019.

p. 28. **'Yet recent decades have witnessed . . .'** Dan Tong, Qiang Zhang, Yixuan Zheng et al., 'Committed Emissions from Existing Energy Infrastructure Jeopardize 1.5°C Climate Target', *Nature* 572 (2019), pp. 373, 374.

p. 28. **Brick by brick, the fireplaces . . .** For an overview of how this works, see Karen C. Seto, Steven J. Davis, Ronald B. Mitchell et al., 'Carbon Lock-In: Types, Causes, and Policy Implications', *Annual Review of Environment and Resources* 41 (2016): 425–52.

p. 30. **Another study from 2018 . . .** Alexander Pfeiffer, Cameron Hepburn, Adrien Vogt-Schilb and Ben Caldecott, 'Committed Emissions from Existing and Planned Power Plants and Asset Stranding Required to Meet the Paris Agreement', *Environmental Research Letters* 13 (2018): 1–11. The findings of this paper are questioned by Christopher J. Smith, Piers M. Forster, Myles Allen et al., 'Current Fossil Fuel Infrastructure Does Not Yet Commit Us to 1.5°C Warming', *Nature Communications* 10 (2019): 1–10.

p. 30. **Yet another found that incumbent . . .** Ottmar Edenhofer, Jan Christoph Steckel, Michael Jakob and Christoph Bertram, 'Reports of Coal's Terminal Decline May Be Exaggerated', *Environmental Research Letters* 2018 (13): 1–9.

p. 30. **'Current investments', the study** . . . Ibid., p. 7.

p. 30. **'policy context'** . . . Seto et al., 'Carbon Lock-In', p. 429.

p. 30. **It comes in two** . . . For a more detailed inventory, written from a pacifist standpoint, see Andrew Fiala, 'Pacifism', *The Stanford Encyclopaedia of Philosophy* (2018), plato.stanford. edu.

p. 31. **No massacre** . . . The poorly executed terrorist action happened to take place when only three worshippers were inside the Al-Noor Islamic Centre, but Philip Manshaus was clearly capable of going on continuous killing sprees; before arriving at the mosque, he had killed his own stepsister (who was of Asian descent). Contrary to what pacifism would demand, Mohammed Rafiq was widely praised as a hero in Norway.

p. 31. **This seems flawed** . . . A classical paper demonstrating the inconsistencies of moral pacifism is Jan Narveson, 'Pacifism: A Philosophical Analysis', *Ethics* 75 (1965): 259–71. A more delightful demolition of moral pacifism is Gerald Runkle, 'Is Violence Always Wrong?', *Journal of Politics* 38 (1976): 367–89.

p. 32. **Among ethical standpoints** . . . Contingent pacifism collapses into just war theory, as pointed out by e.g. Cécile Fabre, 'On Jan Narveson's "Pacifism: A Philosophical Analysis"', *Ethics* 125 (2015), p. 824.

p. 33. **'the leading climate activist'** . . . Hans Baer, 'Activist Profile: Bill McKibben', in Dietz and Garrelts, *Routledge*, p. 223.

p. 33. **'there is a spiritual insight'** . . . Bill McKibben, *Falter: Has the Human Game Begun to Play Itself Out?* (London:

Headline, 2019), p. 220. Emphasis added. Cf. e.g. *Oil and Honey: The Education of an Unlikely Activist* (New York: Times Books/Henry Holt, 2013), p. 15; 'How the Active Many Can Overcome the Ruthless Few', *Nation*, 30 November 2016. A more explicit and comprehensive attempt to ground the climate struggle in moral pacifism of a Christian stamp is Kevin J. O'Brien, *The Violence of Climate Change: Lessons of Resistance from Nonviolent Activists* (Washington, DC: Georgetown University Press, 2017).

p. 33. **According to the adage . . .** Martin Luther King Jr., *A Testament of Hope: The Essential Writings and Speeches* (New York: HarperCollins, 1991), e.g. pp. 18, 41, 219, 466.

p. 34. **Slipping out of the antinomies . . .** On the turn from moral to strategic pacifism, see Mark Engler and Paul Engler, *This Is an Uprising: How Nonviolent Revolt Is Shaping the Twenty-First Century* (New York: Nation Books, 2017).

p. 34. **McKibben now prefers . . .** McKibben, *Falter*, pp. 193, 219; Bill McKibben, 'Foreword', in Engler and Engler, *This*, p. viii.

p. 34. **'the civil resistance model' . . .** Roger Hallam, 'The Civil Resistance Model', in Clare Farrell, Alison Green, Sam Knights and William Skeaping (eds.), *This Is Not a Drill: An Extinction Rebellion Handbook* (London: Penguin, 2019), pp. 100–101. Cf. e.g. Roger Hallam, 'Now We Know: Conventional Campaigning Won't Prevent Our Extinction', *Guardian*, 1 May 2019.

p. 35. **McKibben, for his part . . .** McKibben, 'Foreword', p. viii.

p. 36. **'a whole new wave of comparisons' . . .** Maxine Burkett, 'Climate Disobedience', *Duke Environmental Law and Policy Forum* 27 (2016), p. 2.

p. 36. **The roster of historical analogies begins with slavery . . .** For this analogy, see e.g. ibid., pp. 19–23; Naomi Klein, *This Changes Everything: Capitalism vs. the Climate* (London: Penguin, 2014), pp. 6, 462–64; Andrew Winston, 'The Climate Change Abolitionists', *Guardian*, 27 February 2013; Chris Hayes, 'The New Abolitionism', *Nation*, 22 April 2014; *Climate Home News*, 'Al Gore Likens Climate Movement to Suffrage and Abolition of Slavery', climatechangenews.com, 20 June 2017; Ed Atkinson, 'A Voice from Our History: The 1833 Slavery Abolition Act', *Citizens' Climate Lobby*, citizensclimatelobby.uk, 8 April 2018.

p. 37. **one Oxford professor . . .** Eric Beinhocker, 'I Am a Carbon Abolitionist', *Oxford Martin School*, oxfordmartin.ox.ac.uk, 4 July 2019. Cf. Erich Beinhocker, 'Climate Change Is Morally Wrong. It Is Time for a Carbon Abolition Movement', *Guardian*, 20 September 2019.

p. 37. **Then there were the suffragettes . . .** E.g. Jay Griffiths, 'Courting Arrest', in Farrell et al., *This Is Not*, p. 96; Ronan, '12 Extinction Rebellion Activists Willingly Arrested in Semi-Nude Protest to Highlight Climate Emergency during Brexit Debate in House of Commons', *Extinction Rebellion*, rebellion.earth, 1 April 2019; BBC Radio 4: Beyond Today, 'Are Extinction Rebellion the New

Suffragettes?', bbc.co.uk, 12 April 2019; Natalie Gil, 'Why We Joined Extinction Rebellion AKA the 'New Suffragettes', *Refinery 29*, refinery29.com, 15 April 2019.

p. 37. **One of the most avid arrestees . . .** George Monbiot, 'Today, I Aim to Get Arrested. It Is the Only Real Power Climate Protesters Have', *Guardian*, 16 October 2019.

p. 37. **McKibben has revisited . . .** Bill McKibben, 'The End of Growth', *Mother Jones*, November/December 1999, motherjones.com.

p. 37. **Gandhi was the Einstein . . .** Bill McKibben, 'Gandhi: A Man for All Seasons', *Common Dreams*, 29 December 2007. See further e.g. Cheon and Urpelainen, *Activism*, pp. 41, 83, 155; McKibben, 'Foreword', pp. vii–viii; McKibben, *Falter*, p. 220; Vandana Shiva, 'Foreword', in Farrell et al., *This Is Not*, p. 7; *Economist*, 'Could Extinction Rebellion Be the Next Occupy Movement?', economist.com, 17 April 2019.

p. 38. **Not to forget the US civil rights movement . . .** For this and the other analogies here mentioned, see e.g. Griffiths, 'Courting', p. 96; Danny Burns and Cordula Reimann, 'Movement Building', in Farrell et al., *This Is Not*, pp. 106–68; Cheon and Urpelainen, *Activism*, pp. 94–97; McKibben, *Falter*, p. 224.

p. 38. **'Just as apartheid was the moral issue . . .'** McKibben quoted in Darren Goode, 'McKibben: Sandy "Wake-Up Call" on Climate Change', *Politico*, politico.com, 30 October 2012.

p. 38. **'the same kind of tactic . . .'** McKibben quoted in V. L. Baker, 'Remembering Nelson Mandela and His Fight for

Climate Justice', *Daily Kos*, dailykos.com, 16 December 2013.

p. 39. Slavery was not abolished ... The literature is, of course, enormous. Two seminal works are Robin Blackburn, *The Overthrow of Colonial Slavery, 1776–1848* (London: Verso, 1988); Manisha Sinha, *The Slave's Cause: A History of Abolition* (New Haven: Yale University Press, 2016). The Haitian Revolution is now itself the subject of a vast literature, the classical treatise being C. L. R. James, *The Black Jacobins: Toussaint L'Ouverture and the San Domingo Revolution* (London: Penguin, 2001 [1938]); among later studies, see e.g. the brilliant Carolyn E. Fick, *The Making of Haiti: The Saint Domingue Revolution from Below* (Knoxville: The University of Tennessee Press, 1990). On John Brown, see David S. Reynolds, *John Brown, Abolitionist: The Man Who Killed Slavery, Sparked the Civil War, and Seeded Civil Rights* (New York: Vintage, 2005); quotation from p. 292. For some aspects of the Maroons in the light of the current ecological crisis, see Andreas Malm, 'In Wildness Is the Liberation of the World: On Maroon Ecology and Partisan Nature', *Historical Materialism* 26 (2018): 3–37. McKibben remembers the civil war in *Falter*, p. 218.

p. 39. One of the most prominent ... Robin Blackburn, 'The Role of Slave Resistance in Slave Emancipation', in Seymour Drescher and Pieter C. Emmer (eds.), *Who Abolished Slavery? Slave Revolts and Abolitionism: A Debate with João Pedro Marques* (New York: Berghahn Books, 2010), p. 172.

p. 40. **The suffragettes are instructive ...** Diane Atkinson, *Rise Up, Women! The Remarkable Lives of the Suffragettes* (London: Bloomsbury, 2018).

p. 41. **'To be militant ...'** Quoted in ibid., p. 362.

p. 41. **In a systematic campaign of arson ...** C. J. Bearman, 'An Examination of Suffragette Violence', *English Historical Review* 120 (2005): 365–97.

p. 42. **votes for women, Pankhurst explained ...** Quoted in Atkinson, *Rise Up*, p. 369.

p. 42. **One historian suspects ...** Bearman, 'An Examination', p. 368. The fire is reported in *Manchester Guardian*, 'South Shields Harbour Fire', 26 January 1914.

p. 42. **During this time living in ...** Kathryn Tidrick, *Gandhi: A Political and Spiritual Life* (London: Verso, 2013 [2006]), pp. 56, 66, 73; Mohandas K. Gandhi, *Autobiography: The Story of My Experiments with Truth* (New York: Dover, 1983), p. 313.

p. 43. **'Gandhi famously resisted ...'** O'Brien, *The Violence*, p. 43.

p. 43. **'If I became ...'** Quoted in Domenico Losurdo, 'Moral Dilemmas and Broken Promises: A Historical-Philosophical Overview of the Nonviolent Movement', *Historical Materialism* 18 (2019), p. 96. See further Tidrick, *Gandhi*, pp. 104, 125–32.

p. 44. **Gandhi mightily disapproved ...** See Tidrick, *Gandhi*, e.g. pp. 171, 174–76, 225–26, 232–33, 299–301.

p. 44. **In November 1938 ...** Letter included and analysed in P. R. Kumaraswamy, 'The Jews: Revisiting Mahatma Gandhi's November 1938 Article', *International Studies*

55 (2018): 146–66. On the pathology of pacifism applied to the Third Reich, cf. Ward Churchill, *Pacifism as Pathology: Reflections on the Role of Armed Struggle in North America* (Oakland: AK Press, 2007), pp. 47–52.

p. 44. **Facing objections . . .** Gandhi's subsequent pronouncements on the subject can be found in the section 'Gandhi, the Jews and Zionism', at Jewish Virtual Library, jewish-virtuallibrary.org, from which these quotations are taken. In a saving grace of limited magnitude, Gandhi came out in favour of Palestinian resistance against Zionist colonialism.

p. 45. **'the pre-ordained and potentially divine . . .'** Tidrick, p. xii.

p. 46. **Indeed, so well did they work . . .** Charles E. Cobb Jr., *This Nonviolent Stuff'll Get you Killed: How Guns Made the Civil Rights Movement Possible* (Durham, NC: Duke University Press, 2014).

p. 47. **'Just for self-defense' . . .** Ibid, p. 7.

p. 47. **'What is the best way . . .'** Quotations from ibid., pp. 155, 152.

p. 48. **If the channel of non-violence . . .** 'Letter from Birmingham City Jail' in King, *A Testament*, p. 297.

p. 49. **'Negroes unquestionably . . .'** G. Mennen Williams, assistant secretary of state for African affairs, to Kennedy, quoted in Herbert H. Haines, *Black Radicals and the Civil Rights Mainstream, 1954–1970* (Knoxville: University of Tennessee Press, 1988), p. 161.

p. 49. **In the classical study . . .** Ibid., p. 179. Cf. e.g. Churchill, *Pacifism*, pp. 55–57, 109.

p. 49. **If the cities burned** . . . McGeorge Bundy, quoted in Haines, *Black Radicals*, p. 179.

p. 50. **In the words of Verity Burgmann** . . . Verity Burgmann, 'The Importance of Being Extreme', *Social Alternatives* 37 (2018), p. 10.

p. 51. **'Our policy to achieve . . .'** Nelson Mandela, *Long Walk to Freedom* (London: Abacus, 1995), pp. 433, 320. Mandela describes his disenchantment with non-violence as early as the early 1950s: see pp. 182–83. The South African Communist Party pioneered the break with Gandhian dogma. For an extremely detailed account of the genesis and activities of the MK, see Thula Simpson, *Umkhonto we Sizwe: The ANC's Armed Struggle* (Cape Town: Penguin, 2016).

p. 51. **'Our strategy was . . .'** Mandela, *Long Walk*, p. 336.

p. 52. **Sabotage remained** . . . Gay Seidman, 'Guerrillas in Their Midst: Armed Struggle in the South African Anti-Apartheid Movement', *Mobilization: An International Journal* 6 (2001): 111–27.

p. 52. **'I called for non-violent protest . . .'** Mandela, *Long Walk*, pp. 147, 322. Cf. pp. 183, 351.

p. 55. **At this level of abstraction** . . . Burkett, 'Climate Disobedience', pp. 19–21, 9.

p. 55. **'The arrogance of the authorities . . .'** Hallam, 'The Civil', p. 104.

p. 56. **And yet the 'civil resistance model'** . . . Erica Chenoweth and Maria J. Stephan, *Why Civil Resistance Works: The Strategic Logic of Nonviolent Conflict* (New York: Columbia University Press, 2013). The comparison between Palestine and Slovenia appears on p. 218.

p. 57. **directly engaging an estimated 10 per cent . . .** Charles Kurzman, *The Unthinkable Revolution in Iran* (Cambridge, MA: Harvard University Press, 2004), pp. vii–viii.

p. 58. **The most detailed extant . . .** Misagh Parsa, *Social Origins of the Iranian Revolution* (New Brunswick, NJ: Rutgers University Press, 1989); quotations from pp. 229–30.

p. 59. **'most of the violence . . .'** Michael Axworthy, *Revolutionary Iran: A History of the Islamic Republic* (London: Penguin, 2014), p. 122.

p. 59. **At that point, commandos . . .** Asef Bayat, *Revolution without Revolutionaries: Making Sense of the Arab Spring* (Stanford, CA: Stanford University Press, 2017), p. 32. This was 'the decisive confrontation', in the words of Axworthy, *Revolutionary Iran*, p. 8; the prologue to this book offers a detailed reconstruction of the battle.

p. 59. **Some chapters from this story . . .** For the lore on Egypt, see e.g. Chenoweth and Stephan, *Why Civil*, pp. 6, 229–30; Engler and Engler, *This Is*, pp. 252–60.

p. 59. **'a confrontation that turned peaceful . . .'** M. Cherif Bassiouni, *Chronicle of the Egyptian Revolution and Its Aftermath: 2011–2016* (Oxford: Oxford University Press, 2017), p. 31; see further pp. 291–95.

p. 60. **During the remainder . . .** Neil Ketchley, *Egypt in a Time of Revolution: Contentious Politics and the Arab Spring* (Cambridge: Cambridge University Press, 2017), ch. 2.

p. 60. **'synergetic and complementary'** . . . Ibid., p. 21. Emphasis added.

p. 60. Indeed, Ketchley and his colleague ... Mohammad Ali Kadivar and Neil Ketchley, 'Sticks, Stones, and Molotov Cocktails: Unarmed Collective Violence and Democratization', *Socius: Sociological Research for a Dynamic World* 4 (2018): 1–16.

p. 61. Other scholars have contributed ... E.g. Fabrice Lehoucq, 'Does Nonviolence Work?', *Comparative Politics* 48 (2016): 269–87.

p. 62. From his Birmingham jail ... King, 'Letter from Birmingham', pp. 292–93.

p. 62. 'How much valuable ...' Leon Trotsky, *The Struggle against Fascism in Germany* (New York: Pathfinder, 1971), p. 139.

p. 65. fail to soak up the gases emitted ... See e.g. M. R. Raupach, M. Gloor, J. L. Sarmiento et al., 'The Declining Uptake Rate of Atmospheric CO_2 by Land and Ocean Sinks', *Biogeosciences* 11 (2014): 3453–75.

p. 65. The northern zone of permafrost ... See e.g. Elizabeth M. Herndon, 'Permafrost Slowly Exhales Methane', *Nature Climate Change* 8 (2018): 273–74; Christian Knoblauch, Christian Beer, Susanne Liebner et al., 'Methane Production as Key to the Greenhouse Gas Budget of Thawing Permafrost', *Nature Climate Change* 8 (2018): 309–12; César Plaza, Elaine Pegoraro, Rosvel Bracho et al., 'Direct Observation of Permafrost Degradation and Rapid Soil Carbon Loss in Tundra', *Nature Geoscience* 12 (2019): 627–31.

p. 66. Forest fires work ... See e.g. W. Matt Jolly, Mark A. Cochrane, Patrick H. Freeborn et al., 'Climate-Induced Variations in Global Wildfire Danger from 1979 to

2013', *Nature Communications* 6 (2015): 1–11; Xhante J. Walker, Jennifer L. Baltzer, Steven G. Cumming et al., 'Increasing Wildfires Threaten Historic Carbon Sink of Boreal Forest Soils', *Nature* 572 (2019): 520–23; Zhihua Liu, Ashley P. Ballantyne and L. Annie Cooper, 'Biophysical Feedback of Global Forest Fires on Surface Temperatures', *Nature Communications* 10 (2019): 1–9.

p. 66. **The carbon budgets have yet . . .** See e.g. Jason A. Lowe and Daniel Bernie, 'The Impact of Earth System Feedbacks on Carbon Budgets and Climate Response', *Philosophical Transactions of the Royal Society A* 376 (2018): 1–13; Eleanor J. Burke, Sarah E. Chadburn, Chris Huntingford and Chris D. Jones, 'CO_2 Loss by Permafrost Thawing Implies Additional Reductions to Limit Warming to 1.5 or 2°C', *Environmental Research Letters* 13 (2018): 1–9; Edward Comyn-Platt, Garry Hayman, Chris Huntingford et al., 'Carbon Budgets for 1.5 and 2°C Targets Lowered by Natural Wetland and Permafrost Feedbacks', *Nature Geoscience* 11 (2018): 568–73. See further e.g. Will Steffen, Johan Rockström, Katherine Richardson et al., 'Trajectories of the Earth System in the Anthropocene', *PNAS* 115 (2018): 8252–59; Paul Voosen, 'New Climate Models Forecast a Warming Surge', *Science* 364 (2019): 222–23.

p. 66. **'Even under optimistic assumptions . . .'** J. R. Lamontagne, P. M. Reed, G. Marangoni et al., 'Robust Abatement Pathways to Tolerable Climate Futures Require Immediate Global Action', *Nature Climate Change* 9 (2019), p. 290.

p. 66. **writing in 2019 . . .** Tong et al., 'Committed Emissions', p. 376. Emphasis added. Cf. e.g. the call for a moratorium 'on investments in fossil fuel assets' in Filip Johnsson, Jan Kjärstad and Johan Rootzén, 'The Threat to Climate Change Mitigation Posed by the Abundance of Fossil Fuels', *Climate Policy* 19 (2018), p. 269.

p. 67. **'If we can't get a serious . . .'** McKibben, *Falter*, p. 222. McKibben here quotes Naomi Klein (without specific source).

p. 68. **on one estimate, the instant suspension . . .** Pfeiffer et al., 'Committed Emissions'.

p. 68. **'Sabotage', writes . . .** R. H. Lossin, 'Sabotage as Environmental Activism', *Public Seminar*, 3 July 2018, publicseminar.org. Cf. Jeff Diamanti and Mark Simpson, 'Five Theses on Sabotage in the Shadow of Fossil Capital', *Radical Philosophy* 2.2 (2018): 3–12.

p. 69. **'The current global energy system . . .'** Seto et al., 'Carbon Lock-In', p. 426.

p. 70. **'Protest is when I say . . .'** Ulrike Meinhof, 'From Protest to Resistance', in *Everybody Talks About the Weather . . . We Don't: The Writings of Ulrike Meinhof* (New York: Seven Stories Press, 2008), p. 239.

p. 70. **'Pipelines are very easily sabotaged . . .'** Gal Luft, 'Pipeline Sabotage Is Terrorist's Weapon of Choice', *Pipeline and Gas Journal* 232 (2005): 42–44.

p. 71. **One of the most spectacular actions . . .** The action is described in detail in Simpson, *Umkhonto*, pp. 267–69. Actions again targeted Sasol facilities in 1981 and in 1985: see ibid., pp. 284–85, 363–64.

p. 71. **'shattered the myth of white . . .'** Ginwala quoted in Lee Jones, *Societies Under Siege: Exploring How International Economic Sanctions (Do Not) Work* (Oxford: Oxford University Press, 2015), p. 68.

p. 71. **In the assessment of Mandela . . .** Mandela, *Long Walk*, p. 603.

p. 71. **'None of these attacks . . .'** Seidman, 'Guerrillas', p. 118. Emphasis in original.

p. 71. **In the wake of the First World War . . .** On the pipeline and its place in the revolt of 1936–39, see e.g. Rachel Havrelock, 'The Borders Beneath: On Pipelines and Resource Sovereignty', *South Atlantic Quarterly* 116 (2017): 408–16; Matthew Hughes, 'Terror in the Galilee: British-Jewish Collaboration and the Special Night Squads in Palestine during the Arab Revolt, 1938–9', *Journal of Imperial and Commonwealth History* 43 (2015): 590–610; Steven Pressfield, *The Lion's Gate: On the Front Lines of the Six Day War* (New York: Penguin, 2015), p. 77.

p. 72. **'unable to defend this . . .'** Ghassan Kanafani, *The 1939–39 Revolt in Palestine* (New York: Committee for a Democratic Palestine, 1972), p. 58.

p. 72. **Sabotage along the same lines . . .** Zachary Davis Cuyler, 'Toward the Target and the Goal: Infrastructure Sabotage and Palestinian Liberation in the Pages of *Al-Hadaf*', *Historical Materialism*, forthcoming.

p. 73. **After the non-violent movement . . .** Cyril Obi and Siri Aas Rustad (eds.), *Oil and Insurgency in the Niger Delta* (London: Zed, 2011); Freedom C. Onuoha, 'Oil

Pipeline Sabotage in Nigeria: Dimensions, Actors and Implications for National Security', *African Security Studies* 17 (2008): 99–115; Michael Watts, 'Petro-Insurgency or Criminal Syndicate? Conflict and Violence in the Niger Delta', *Review of African Political Economy* 34 (2007): 637–60.

p. 73. **'a fantastically audacious . . .'** Watts, 'Petro-Insurgency', p. 645.

p. 74. **'The stable and regularised flow . . .'** Ibid.

p. 74. **During the Egyptian revolution** ... Bassiouni, *Chronicle*, pp. 301, 580.

p. 74. **In India, the Naxalites** ... Utpal Bhaskar, 'Naxals Put the Squeeze on Transport of Jharkhand Coal', *LiveMint*, livemint.com, 1 December 2019; Ruchira Singh, 'Maoist Threat Hampering India Coal Output – Minister', Reuters, reuters.com, 23 June 2010; Ruchira Singh and Krittivas Mukherjee, 'Govt Clamps Down on Maoists to Woo Investors', Reuters, 3 August 2010; Shivani Gite, 'Maoists Blow Up Diesel Tanker in Chhattisgarh, Three Dead', *Track*, newstracklive.com, 24 September 2019; FP Staff, 'Gadchiroli Naxal Attack Today, Updates: 15 Security Personnel, Driver Killed; Sharad Pawar Demands CM's Resignation', *Firstpost*, firstpost.com, 1 May 2019; IANS, 'Jharkhand: Maoists Set 16 Vehicles Ablaze, Assault Six Labourers', *India Today*, indiatoday. in, 12 July 2019.

p. 75. **According to a chorus** ... Martin Chulov, 'Middle East Drones Signal End to Era of Fast Jet Air Supremacy', *Guardian*, 16 September 2019; P. W. Singer, 'The

Future of War Is Already Here', *New York Times*, 18 September 2019.

p. 75. 'stark evidence of the vulnerability . . .' Anthony Diapola and Verity Radcliffe, 'Saudi Attacks Reveal Oil Supply Fragility in Asymmetric War', *Bloomberg*, bloomberg.com, 15 September 2019.

p. 76. far higher than in the North, according to some polls . . . E.g. Hanno Sandvik, 'Public Concern over Global Warming Correlates Negatively with National Wealth', *Climatic Change* 90 (2008): 333–41; So Young Kim and Yael Wolinsky-Nahmias, 'Cross-National Public Opinion on Climate Change: Effects of Affluence and Vulnerability', *Global Environmental Politics* 14 (2014): 79–106; Alex Y. Lo and Alex T. Chow, 'The Relationship Between Climate Change Concern and National Wealth', *Climatic Change* 131 (2015): 335–48.

p. 76. Not only did he revamp . . . See Robert Springborg, 'Egypt: The Challenge of Squaring the Energy– Environment–Growth Triangle', in Robert E. Looney (ed.), *Routledge Handbook of Transitions in Energy and Climate Security* (Abingdon, UK: Routledge, 2017): 272–84.

p. 77. Few countries have seen a similar recent spurt . . . Edenhofer et al., 'Reports of Coal's', pp. 4, 7.

p. 78. Western Europe had its own moment . . . Brynjar Lia and Åshild Kjøk, 'Energy Supply as Terrorist Targets? Patterns of "Petroleum Terrorism" 1968–99', in Daniel Heradstveit and Helge Hveem (eds.), *Oil in the Gulf: Obstacles to Democracy and Development* (Aldershot, UK: Ashgate, 2004), pp. 105–6, 109, 114, 120–21.

p. 79. During the so-called refugee crisis . . . AFP, 'Increase in Arson at German Refugee Centres: Police', *Local*, thelocal.de, 14 May 2016.

p. 80. and launched a blog . . . The blog is still up: asfaltsdjungelnsindianer.wordpress.com.

p. 82. 'exceedingly SUV-dense quarters' . . . Isabella Iverius, '"Vi pyser däck för miljöns skull"', *Dagens Nyheter*, 9 September 2007.

p. 83. 'some Indian to bathe . . .' Redaktionen, 'Asfaltsdjungelns indianer kanske lever farligt', *Motor Life Today*, motor-life.com, September 2007.

p. 84. Announcing a 'ceasefire' . . . The 'ceasefire' was announced in Asfaltsdjungelns indianer, '"Nu tar vi indianer en paus"', *Aftonbladet*, aftonbladet.se, 10 December 2007.

p. 85. It has been demonstrated . . . See e.g. Emily Huddart Kennedy, Harvey Krahn and Naomi T. Krogman, 'Egregious Emitters: Disproportionality in Household Carbon Footprints', *Environment and Behavior* 46 (2014): 535–55; Dominik Wiedenhofer, Dabo Guan, Zhu Liu et al., 'Unequal Household Carbon Footprints in China', *Nature Climate Change* 7 (2017): 75–80; Kyle W. Knight, Juliet B. Schor and Andrew K. Jorgensen, 'Wealth Inequality and Carbon Emissions in High-Income Countries', *Social Currents* 4 (2017): 403–12; Klaus Hubacek, Giovanni Baiocchi, Kuishuang Feng et al., 'Global Carbon Inequality', *Energy, Ecology and Environment* 2 (2017): 361–69.

p. 85. 'unequal ability to pollute' . . . Dario Kenner, *Carbon Inequality: The Role of the Richest in Climate Change*

(Abingdon, UK: Routledge, 2019), p. 12. Emphasis removed.

p. 85. *'all rich individuals'* ... Ibid., p. 17. Emphasis in original.

p. 86. **One Oxfam report from 2015** ... Oxfam, *Extreme Carbon Inequality*, oxfam.org, 2 December 2015.

p. 86. **One article published by** ... Ilona M. Otto, Kyoung Mi Kim, Nika Dubrovsky and Wolfgang Lucht, 'Shift the Focus from the Super-Poor to the Super-Rich', *Nature Climate Change* 9 (2019): 82–87.

p. 86. **Another study from the same year** ... Michael J. Lynch, Michael A. Long, Paul B. Stretesky and Kimberly L. Barrett, 'Measuring the Ecological Impact of the Wealthy: Excessive Consumption, Ecological Disorganization, Green Crime, and Justice', *Social Currents* 6 (2019): 377–95.

p. 86. **One single flight from** ... Niko Kommenda, 'How Your Flight Emits as Much CO_2 as Many People Do in a Year', *Guardian*, 19 July 2019.

p. 87. **Even in such a flying-prone country** ... Niko Kommenda, '1% of English Residents Take One-Fifth of Overseas Flights, Survey Shows', *Guardian*, 25 September 2019.

p. 87. **But the super-rich prefer** ... Dario Kenner, 'Inequality of Overconsumption: The Ecological Footprint of the Richest', Anglia Ruskin University and Global Sustainability Institute, working paper, November 2015, p. 6.

p. 87. **The private jets operating in the US** ... Lynch et al., 'Measuring', p. 389.

p. 87. **'Can we really equate'** ... Anil Agarwal and Sunita Narain, *Global Warming in an Unequal World: A Case of Environmental Colonialism* (New Delhi: Centre for Science and Environment, 1991), p. 3. Emphasis removed.

p. 87. **This insight was then picked up** ... Henry Shue, 'Subsistence Emissions and Luxury Emissions', *Law and Policy* 15 (1993): 39–59; reprinted in Henry Shue, *Climate Justice: Vulnerability and Protection* (Oxford: Oxford University Press, 2014), ch. 2.

p. 88. **The former happen because rich people** ... See also the excellent discussion in Wouter Peeters, Andries De Smet, Lisa Diependaele and Sigrid Sterckx, *Climate Change and Individual Responsibility: Agency, Moral Disengagement and the Motivational Gap* (Basingstoke, UK: Palgrave Macmillan, 2015), pp. 29–32.

p. 88. **'People don't need yachts ...'** Phil Popham quoted in Kenner, *Carbon*, p. 18.

p. 88. **'is to discard the most fundamental ...'** Shue, 'Subsistence Emissions', p. 55.

p. 88. **'We ought', he contended** ... Shue, *Climate*, p. 7.

p. 88. **'even in an emergency ...'** Ibid., p. 46.

p. 88. **This argument was conceived** ... See Shue, 'Subsistence Emissions', pp. 42, 56–58; Shue, *Climate*, p. 46; Henry Shue, 'Subsistence Protection and Mitigation Ambition: Necessities, Economic and Climatic', *British Journal of Politics and International Relations* 21 (2019): 255–56.

p. 89. **If, back in the 1990s** ... See Shue, *Climate*, pp. 328–31; Shue, 'Subsistence Protection', pp. 255–57; Alex McLaughlin, 'Justifying Subsistence Emissions, Past and

Present', *British Journal of Politics and International Relations* 21 (2019): 263–69.

p. 89. **'No one, rich or poor'** . . . Shue, *Climate*, p. 7.

p. 89. **Luckily, this does not condemn** . . . Ibid., p. 329.

p. 90. **First, the harm they inflict** . . . Cf. e.g. David Schlosberg, 'Further Uses for the Luxury/Subsistence Distinction: Impacts, Ceilings, and Adaptation', *British Journal of Politics and International Relations* 21 (2019): 298–99; John Nolt, 'Casualties as a Moral Measure of Climate Change', *Climatic Change* 130 (2015): 347–58; Peeters et al., *Climate Change*, p. 52.

p. 90. **A group of American and British** . . . Lynch et al., 'Measuring', p. 378; and with greater elaboration, Michael J. Lynch, Michael A. Long, Kimberley L. Barrett and Paul B. Stretesky, 'Is It a Crime to Produce Ecological Disorganization? Why Green Criminology and Political Economy Matter in the Analysis of Global Ecological Harms', *British Journal of Criminology* 53 (2013): 997–1016.

p. 90. **It is aggravated by the circumstance** . . . Cf. Kenner, *Carbon*, pp. 18–19; Otto et al., 'Shift the Focus', p. 82.

p. 90. **not only maintaining but** . . . Cf. Otto et al., 'Shift the Focus', pp. 82–83; Lynch et al., 'Is It a Crime', p. 1005.

p. 91. **the original insight holds** . . . Cf. Shue, 'Subsistence Protection', p. 257; McLaughlin, 'Justifying', p. 266.

p. 92. **A peasant who emits CH_4** . . . Cf. Peeters et al., *Climate Change*, p. 120.

p. 92. **'compulsory restrictions . . .'** Otto et al., 'Shift the Focus', p. 83.

p. 93.   **Nor is this crime likely** . . . Lynch et al., 'Is It a Crime', p. 998; Lynch et al., 'Measuring', p. 390.

p. 93.   **'so owning a car is essential'** . . . Didier Fassin and Anne-Claire Defossez, 'An Improbable Movement? Macron's France and the Rise of the Gilets Jaunes', *New Left Review* 2.115 (2019): 79.

p. 94.   **And so we might take a leaf from the Fedaiyan** . . . Amir Parviz Pouyan, *On the Necessity of Armed Struggle and Refutation of the Theory of 'Survival'* (New York: Support Committee for the Iranian People's Struggles, 1977), quotations from pp. 42, 35–36.

p. 96.   **SUVs first seized the US** . . . AP, '2016 U.S. Auto Sales Set a New Record High, Led by SUVs', *Los Angeles Times*, latimes.com, 4 January 2017. Sales dropped slightly in 2017.

p. 96.   **In Europe, the 'Chelsea tractors'** . . . Transport and Environment, *Mission Possible: How Car Makers Can Reach Their CO_2 Targets and Avoid Fines* (Brussels: Transport and Environment, 2019), e.g. pp. 3, 18–20; Laura Laker, ' "A Deadly Problem": Should We Ban SUVs from Our Cities?', *Guardian*, 7 October 2019.

p. 96.   **But the movement is on their track** . . . Matthew Robinson, 'Frankfurt Motor Show Hit by Huge Climate Protests', *CNN*, 15 September 2019.

p. 96.   **It came on the heels of a series** . . . Philip Oltermann, 'Berliners Call for 4X4 Ban after Four People Killed in Collision', *Guardian*, 9 September 2019; Laker, ' "A Deadly Problem" '.

p. 97.   **On the night when Donald Trump** . . . This follows the account provided by Reznicek and Montoya themselves in their press release. 'Ruby Montoya & Jessica Reznicek: DAPL Ecosabotage Press Release', *Stop Fossil Fuels*, stop-fossilfuels.org, 24 July 2016. Cf. e.g. Anna Spoerre, 'Women Who "Sabotaged" Dakota Access Pipeline Charged Almost 3 Years after Damages First Reported', *Des Moines Register*, eu.desmoinesregister.com, 1 October 2019.

p. 97. Reznicek and Montoya had immersed themselves . . . See e.g. Alleen Brown, 'Dakota Access Pipeline Activists Face 110 Years in Prison, Two Years after Confessing Sabotage', *Intercept*, 4 October 2019.

p. 98. After exploring and exhausting all avenues . . . 'Ruby Montoya & Jessica Reznicek: DAPL'.

p. 98. Their sabotage delayed construction . . . Cf. 'Ruby Montoya & Jessica Reznicek: DAPL Ecosaboteurs', *Stop Fossil Fuels*, stopfossilfuels.org, n.d.

p. 98. In Germany, the conflict over the Hambach forest . . . See e.g. AFP, 'German Police Confront Treehouse Activists after Six-Year Standoff', *Guardian*, 13 September 2018; AP/DPA, 'Arson Attacks on German Companies Linked to Hambach Forest Protest?', *Deutsche Welle*, dw.com, 4 October 2018; AFP, 'Thousands of Anti-coal Protesters Celebrate German Forest's Reprieve', *Guardian*, 6 October 2018.

p. 100. 'The oil being taken out of the ground . . .' Jessica Reznicek on *Democracy Now!*, 28 July 2017, YouTube.

p. 100. 'a whip of cords' . . . John 2:15.

p. 100. It has been argued . . . E.g. Runkle, 'Is Violence', p. 370.

p. 101. **One much-cited philosophical essay . . .** Robert Audi, 'On the Meaning and Justification of Violence', in Jerome A. Shaffer, *Violence: Award-Winning Essays in the Council for Philosophical Studies Competition* (New York: David McKay, 1971), quotations from pp. 50, 59. Emphases in original. For an excellent contemporary discussion, see Vittorio Bufacchi, 'Two Concepts of Violence', *Political Studies Review* 3 (2005): 193–204. Note that we here leave out the question of psychological, structural, slow and other broadly conceived forms of violence.

p. 101. **In a similar vein, Ted . . .** Ted Honderich, *Terrorism for Humanity: Inquiries in Political Philosophy* (London: Pluto, 2003), p. 15 (also on p. 154).

p. 101. **Chenoweth and Stephan submit . . .** Chenoweth and Stephan, *Why Civil*, p. 13.

p. 101. **But strategic pacifists are right . . .** This is argued by e.g. Engler and Engler, *This Is*, p. 236.

p. 102. **But in the very same breath . . .** This paragraph and the next draw on N. P. Adams, 'Uncivil Disobedience: Political Commitment and Violence', *Res Publica* 24 (2018): 487–89; John Morreall, 'The Justifiability of Violent Civil Disobedience', *Canadian Journal of Philosophy* 6 (1976): 38; Steve Vanderheiden, 'Eco-terrorism of Justified Resistance? Radical Environmentalism and the "War on Terror"', *Politics and Society* 33 (2005): 431; Runkle, 'Is Violence', p. 370.

p. 102. **'Violent they certainly were . . .'** Martin Luther King Jr., 'The Trumpet of Conscience', in King, *A Testament*, p. 649.

p. 104. **'Is not a woman's life . . .'** Pankhurst quoted in Atkinson, *Rise Up*, p. 288.

p. 104. **Or, in the words of one philosopher . . .** Morreall, 'The Justifiability', p. 43.

p. 105. **William Smith, one of the most astute . . .** William Smith, 'Disruptive Democracy: The Ethics of Direct Action', *Raisons politiques* no. 69 (2018), quotations from pp. 13, 22, 24.

p. 106. **There is nothing madly aberrant . . .** Cf. e.g. Morreall, 'The Justifiability'; Vanderheiden, 'Eco-terrorism'; Adams, 'Uncivil Disobedience'; Simo Kyllönen, 'Civil Disobedience: Climate Protests and a Rawlsian Argument for "Atmospheric" Fairness', *Environmental Values* 23 (2014): 593–613. For sophisticated analyses even more generous about the right to use revolutionary violence, primarily in the struggle against foreign occupations, see Christopher J. Finlay, *Terrorism and the Right to Resist: A Theory of Just Revolutionary War* (Cambridge: Cambridge University Press, 2015); Michael L. Gross, *The Ethics of Insurgency: A Critical Guide to Guerrilla Warfare* (Cambridge: Cambridge University Press, 2015).

p. 107. **Few other concepts are as loaded . . .** See e.g. Finlay, *Terrorism*, pp. 5, 100, 247; Gross, *Ethics*, pp. 155–56; Christopher J. Finlay, 'How to Do Things with the Word "Terrorist"', *Review of International Studies* 35 (2009): 751–74.

p. 107. **On this definition, it would be . . .** This draws on Vanderheiden, 'Eco-terrorism', e.g. pp. 427, 432, 436, 440.

p. 108. **'climate terrorism is on the horizon'** ... Sara Malm, 'Experter varnar: Desperata klimataktivister kan ta till terrorism', *Expressen*, expressen.se, 18 May 2019.

p. 108. **'One can easily imagine ...'** Peter Viggo Jakobsen in Simone Skyum, 'Eksperter frygter vold og terror fra frustrerede klimaaktivister', *Jyllands-Posten*, jyllands-posten. dk, 18 May 2019.

p. 108. **'a categorically distinct act'** ... Ibid., p. 432.

p. 109. **In 2004, two scholars working for** ... Lya and Kjøk, 'Energy Supply', quotation from p. 116.

p. 110. **When the townships boiled** ... Mandela, *Long Walk*, pp. 322, 337. It would be historically dishonest, however, to hide the fact that the MK moved beyond sabotage. Mandela describes how its first car bombing in May 1983, targeting an air force and military intelligence office, killed 19 and injured 200 people. 'The killing of civilians was a tragic accident, and I felt a profound horror at the death toll. But disturbed as I was by these casualties, I knew that such accidents were the inevitable consequence of the decision to embark on a military struggle. Human fallibility is always a part of war, and the price of it is always high. It was precisely because we knew that such incidents would occur that our decision to take up arms had been so grave and reluctant. But as Oliver [Tambo] said at the time of the bombing, the apartheid struggle was imposed upon us by the violence of the apartheid regime.' Ibid., pp. 617–18.

p. 111. **'not to endanger life ...'** Ibid., p. 337; Smith, 'Disruptive', pp. 18–19. Cf. Vanderheiden, 'Eco-terrorism', pp. 441, 445.

p. 111. **The first part of his response presented . . .** 'If you're an oil company, whom would you rather fight? A guy with a rifle is no problem; you've got access to all the rifles in the world. But a guy with some solar panels, access to social media, and a clever streak will drive you three kinds of nuts.' McKibben, *Falter*, p. 225. As if oil companies didn't have energy sources, access to social media and intelligence. Cf. e.g. Engler and Engler, *This Is*, pp. 6, 237–38.

p. 113. **'We live in a dream world . . .'** George Monbiot, 'With Eyes Wide Shut', *Guardian*, 12 August 2003. For a nuanced discussion of the objection from time, see Gross, *The Ethics*, pp. 265–67.

p. 114. **'barriers to participation . . .'** Chenoweth and Stephan, *Why Civil*, p. 10. Cf. e.g. pp. 30–37; Engler and Engler, *This Is*, pp. 26, 246–47.

p. 115. **In the handbook, we learn . . .** J. S. Rafaeli with Neil Woods, 'Fighting the Wrong War', in Farrell et al., *This Is Not*, p. 41; Griffiths, 'Courting', p. 96.

p. 115. **As pointed out in an open letter to XR ...** The Wretched of the Earth, Argentina Solidarity Campaign, Black Lives Matter UK et al., 'An Open Letter to Extinction Rebellion', *Red Pepper*, redpepper.org.uk, 3 May 2019. Cf. Damien Gayle, 'Does Extinction Rebellion Have a Race Problem?', *Guardian*, 4 October 2019.

p. 116. **Taken from the reading of movements . . .** See e.g. Chenoweth and Stephan, *Why Civil*, pp. 60–61, 202–7.

p. 116. **It loses the rest when we consider only . . .** Adams, 'Uncivil', p. 489.

p. 117. **As soon as violence is thrown into the mix . . .** For some research corroborating this view, see Brent Simpson, Robb Willer and Matthew Feinberg, 'Does Violent Protest Backfire? Testing a Theory of Public Reactions to Activist Violence', *Socius: Sociological Research for a Dynamic World* 4 (2018): 1–14; Jordi Muñoz and Eva Anduiza, ' "If a Fight Starts, Watch the Crowd": The Effect of Violence on Popular Support for Social Movements', *Journal of Peace Research* 56 (2019): 485–98.

p. 117. **the American allergy . . .** The classical text here is Churchill, *Pacifism*.

p. 119. **The task of climate activists cannot be . . .** Cf. Mike Ryan, 'On Ward Churchill's "Pacifism as Pathology": Toward a Revolutionary Practice', in Churchill, *Pacifism*, p. 129.

p. 120. **The same temporality may swiftly move . . .** Thus Bill McKibben has been analysed as the representative of a radical flank in American climate politics in the late 2010s, in Todd Schifeling and Andrew J. Hoffman, 'Bill McKibben's Influence on U.S. Climate Change Discourse: Shifting Field-Level Debates through Radical Flank Effects', *Organization & Environment* 32 (2019): 213–33.

p. 120. **'a division of labor . . .'** Haines, *Black Radicals*, p. 184. Cf. e.g. pp. 2–4, 8–9, 65–66, 180–83.

p. 121. **'community of opinion'** ... Smith, 'Disruptive', pp. 17–18, 20–21. Cf. Finlay, *Terrorism*, p. 309.

p. 122. **In October 2019, Jessica Reznicek** ... Brown, 'Dakota Access'.

p. 122. **The previous year, a panel at a conference** ... Tom DiChristopher, 'Pipeline CEOs Vow to Fight Back against Environmental Activism and Sabotage', CNBC, cnbc.com, 9 March 2018.

p. 122. **'high levels of both commitment ...'** Chenoweth and Stephan, *Why Civil*, p. 37.

p. 123. **Indeed, if one wants to accomplish something** ... Damien Gayle, 'Heathrow Third Runway Activists Arrested before Drone Protest', *Guardian*, 13 September 2019.

p. 123. **in August 2018, for example, an activist paddling** ... Susie Cagle, ' "Protesters as Terrorists": Growing Number of States Turn Anti-Pipeline Activism into a Crime', *Guardian*, 8 July 2019.

p. 125. **the official statement exonerated the kick-to-the-head** ... Extinction Rebellion, 'Statement on Today's Tube Action', *Extinction Rebellion*, rebellion.earth, 17 October 2019.

p. 126. **as one *Guardian* columnist quipped** ... Catherine Bennett, 'The Extinction Rebels Have a Noble Cause. What They Don't Need Now Is Tactical Stupidity', *Guardian*, 20 October 2019.

p. 127. **'If you believe', says one** ... This follows Salvage Editorial Collective, 'Tragedy of the Worker: Toward the Proletarocene', *Salvage* 7 (2019): 40–1.

p. 133. **One of them is Roy . . .** Roy Scranton, *Learning to Die in the Anthropocene: Reflections on the End of a Civilization* (San Francisco: City Lights, 2015), quotations from pp. 16–17; Roy Scranton, *We're Doomed. Now What? Essays on War and Climate Change* (New York: Soho Press, 2018), quotations from pp. 7, 73. For an excellent critique of Scranton, from which this text has borrowed half of its subtitle, see Ted Stolze, 'Against Climate Stoicism: Learning to Fight in the Anthropocene', in Jan Jagodzinski (ed.), *Interrogating the Anthropocene: Ecology, Aesthetics, Pedagogy and the Future in Question* (Cham, Switzerland: Palgrave Macmillan, 2018), pp. 317–37.

p. 133. **It 'ends in disaster . . .'** Roy Scranton, 'No Happy Ending: On Bill McKibben's "Falter" and David Wallace-Wells's "The Uninhabitable Earth" ', *Los Angeles Review of Books*, lareviewofbooks.org, 3 June 2019.

p. 134. **He describes the vacuous . . .** Scranton, *Learning*, p. 62.

p. 134. **There is no way a movement . . .** Ibid., p. 60.

p. 134. **In an essay published in the *Los Angeles* . . .** Scranton, 'No Happy'.

p. 134. **For one brief moment . . .** Scranton, *Learning*, 74.

p. 135. **'If the bad news we must confront . . .'** Scranton, *We're Doomed*, pp. 68, 8, 316–17; *Learning*, pp. 84–85.

p. 135. **He is an introspective . . .** Scranton, *We're Doomed*, pp. 90, 66, 69; *Learning*, pp. 68, 85.

p. 136. **As a young man in Oregon . . .** Scranton, 'No Happy'; *We're Doomed*, pp. 90–95 ('the dirty work of empire': here quoting George Orwell).

p. 137. **'Those brutal, maddening days ...'** Scranton, *We're Doomed*, pp. 97, 140.

p. 137. **He had to give up 'the fragile ...'** Scranton, *We're Doomed*, pp. 129, 201, 203.

p. 138. **Mitigating global heating ...** This analogy is made in Scranton, 'No Happy'.

p. 138. **he even calls for 'socialist revolution' ...** Scranton, *We're Doomed*, p. 333; cf. pp. 320, 330–31. Speaking of conflicted intellect, Scranton informs us that 'global capitalist civilization as we know it is already over'. Scranton, *Learning*, p. 24.

p. 138. **Like Scranton, he believes ...** Jonathan Franzen, *The End of the End of the World* (London: 4th Estate, 2018), p. 52; Jonathan Franzen, 'What If We Stopped Pretending?', *New Yorker*, newyorker.com, 8 September 2019.

p. 139. **Franzen, like Scranton, feels guilty ...** Franzen, *The End*, pp. 44, 51.

p. 139. **And this human nature is not ...** Franzen, 'What if'.

p. 139. **'what makes intuitive moral sense' ...** Franzen, *The End*, p. 51. Emphasis added.

p. 139. **'bigger than World War II, bigger ...'** Scranton, 'No Happy'. Emphasis added.

p. 140. **'brilliant adapters; climate change is just the same ...'** Franzen, *The End*, p. 53. Cf. Franzen's musings on the adaptability of birds, which seems to mirror that of prosperous Americans, on p. 48.

p. 141. **As another climate philosopher ...** Catriona McKinnon, 'Climate Change: Against Despair', *Ethics and the Environment* 19 (2014): 31–48.

p. 141. 'radically reorient all human economic . . .' Scranton, *We're Doomed*, p. 320. Emphasis added.

p. 142. 'it may become a self-fulfilling prophecy . . .' McKinnon, 'Climate', p. 45.

p. 143. 'and not give up' . . . Ibid., pp. 41, 43.

p. 144. 'until we reach a point . . .' Ibid., p. 40.

p. 145. 'It is not a question of . . .' Lamontagne et al., 'Robust Abatement', p. 290.

p. 145. 'The precise level of future warming . . .' Tong et al., 'Committed Emissions', p. 376.

p. 146. 'The fight is, definitely, not yet lost . . .' David Wallace-Wells, *The Uninhabitable Earth* (London: Allen Lane, 2019), p. 32.

p. 147. 'The context for hope . . .' McKinnon, 'Climate', p. 40.

p. 147. 'anything could happen . . .' Rebecca Solnit, *Hope in the Dark: Untold Histories, Wild Possibilities* (Edinburgh: Canongate, 2016), pp. 4, 22.

p. 148. 'convince youths to stop . . .' Chenoweth and Stephan, *Why Civil*, p. 120; see further pp. 119–46.

p. 148. She was a lead officer . . . Maria J. Stephan, United States Institute of Peace, usip.org, accessed 15 October 2019; Bureau of Conflict and Stabilization Operations, U.S. Department of State, state.gov, accessed 15 October 2019.

p. 148. 'a pretext for purging' . . . Chenoweth and Stephan, *Why Civil*, p. 117.

p. 149. But this 'success condition' . . . The success condition and the Warsaw uprising are discussed in Daniel Statman, 'On the Success Condition for Legitimate Self-Defense', *Ethics* 118 (2008): 659–86.

p. 149. **hothouse Earth scenario** ... See Steffen et al., 'Trajectories of the Earth'.

p. 150. **In the ghettos, as in the extermination camps** ... Alain Brossat and Sylvie Klingberg, *Revolutionary Yiddishland: A History of Jewish Radicalism* (London: Verso, 2016), p. 162. Emphasis added.

p. 150. **to vindicate the fundamental values of life** ... This is one of the solutions to the problem of the success condition considered in Statman, 'On the Success', although he ultimately rejects vindication in favour of the protection of *honour* as the meaning of hopeless resistance.

p. 151. **Defeat also has a pedagogical** ... As pointed out by Jennifer Hadden, 'Learning from Defeat: The Strategic Reorientation of the U.S. Climate Movement', in Cassegård et al., *Climate*, p. 145.

p. 151. **'bourgeois luxury'** ... Jonas Gren, 'Vad vet författarna om klimathotet som vetenskapen har missat?', *Dagens Nyheter*, 10 September 2019.

p. 151. **'OMG, I am the destruction ...'** Scranton, *We're Doomed*, pp. 46–47.

p. 152. **Their campaigns of 'monkeywrenching' or 'ecotage'** ... For this aspect of the movement, see e.g. Adam Weissman, 'The Revolution in Everyday Life', in Steven Best and Anthony J. Nocella (eds.), *Igniting a Revolution: Voices in Defense of the Earth* (Oakland: AK Press, 2006), pp. 127–36.

p. 153. **'predicated on perpetual growth'** ... Aric McBay, Lierre Keith and Derrick Jensen, *Deep Green Resistance:*

Strategy to Save the Planet (New York: Seven S
2011), p. 209. Emphasis removed.

p. 153. 'A truly sustainable number . . .' Ibid., p. 210. Cf. e
pp. 194, 441.

p. 153. The EF!, ALF, ELF and loosely associated . . . Michael Loadenthal, '"Eco-Terrorism": An Incident-Driven History of Attack (1973–2010)', *Journal for the Study of Radicalism* 11 (2017): 1–104. On the wide range of attacks, see further Best and Nocella, *Igniting*.

p. 154. In 1996, ELF glued the locks . . . Noel Molland, 'A Spark That Ignited a Flame: The Evolution of the Earth Liberation Front', in Best and Nocella, *Igniting*, pp. 55–57.

p. 154. In 2003, ELF cells claimed responsibility . . . Julie Tamaki, Jia-Rui Chong and Mitchell Landsberg, 'Radicals Target SUVs in Series of Southland Attacks', *Los Angeles Times*, latimes.com, 23 August 2003. The ELF supplies the empirical material to the conceptual discussion in Vanderheiden, 'Eco-terrorism'.

p. 154. Loadenthal highlights the fact . . . Loadenthal, '"Eco-Terrorism"', pp. 4–5, 8, 17. Cf. Vanderheiden, 'Eco-terrorism', p. 426.

p. 155. 'Houses were checked . . .' ELF, 'Earth Liberation Front FAQ', in Best and Nocella, *Igniting*, p. 407.

p. 155. 'It is our prediction that there . . .' McBay et al., *Deep Green*, pp. 26, 494.

p. 156. as long as the 'warriors' . . . Ibid., pp. 299, 506.

p. 156. Jensen has also proposed 'immediately . . .' Derrick Jensen, 'What Goes Up Must Come Down', in Best and Nocella, *Igniting*, p. 289.

...ad industrial collapse . . .' McBay et ... p. 458.

...able individuals make uniquely . . .'

...tion, media, politicians were ... ...om *Die Nachrichten*, 'Ende im Lausitzer ... utschlandfunk.de, 15 May 2016; *RBB 24*, 'Viel Kritik nach Kohle-Protestwochenende in der Lausitz', rbb24.de, 17 May 2016; TT, 'Fridolin tar avstånd från kolprotest', *Sydsvenska Dagbladet*, 16 May 2016 (CEO: Hartmuth Zeiss; mayor: Christine Herntier; public broadcaster: *RBB 24*).

p. 161. **More violence of that kind . . .** See Andreas Malm and The Zetkin Collective, *White Skin, Black Fuel: On the Danger of Fossil Fascism* (London: Verso, 2021).

p. 161. **There is a famous line in . . .** Frantz Fanon, *The Wretched of the Earth* (London: Penguin, 2001 [1961]), p. 74.

Acknowledgements

The ideas in this text are solely my responsibility. So are any oversights and misjudgements. My ideas have, however, developed through intense conversations with comrades in the movement over the past years. Thanks to Tadzio, Lise, Viktor, Anna, Thea, Gabriel, comrades at Code Rood, Klimacamp Leipziger Land, Folk mot fossilgas and many others. Special thanks to Lise, Viktor and Troy, who read the manuscript and gave critical comments. Special thanks also to my wonderful affinity group, with whom I have had the privilege of doing actions in recent years. Thanks to Jessie and Sebastian at Verso and Stella and Jean at La Fabrique. To Blanck Mass for *Animated Violence Mild*. To Atousa, Shahrokh, Farahnaz and Shokoh jun for their generosity and hospitality. To Shora for everything, still, and to Latifa. This one is for Nadim Walter Thaer.